Foundation
in
Accounting

1

This volume covers the first part of the Foundation or Introductory Course in Accounting for students of accounting and business studies.

Volume 2 will include material for the remainder of the first year and will contain some topics which may be taught in the second year.

It is planned to extend the series to span the more advanced topics of professional and academic studies.

Foundation in Accounting 1

RICHARD LEWIS
IAN GILLESPIE

Department of Accountancy & Taxation
School of Business Studies
City of London Polytechnic

Prentice/Hall International, Inc., London

ISBN 0-13-329730-6

Prentice-Hall International, Inc., *London*
Prentice-Hall of Australia Pty. Ltd., *Sydney*
Prentice-Hall of Canada, Ltd., *Toronto*
Prentice-Hall of India Private Limited, *New Delhi*
Prentice-Hall of Japan, Inc., *Tokyo*
Prentice-Hall of Southeast Asia Pte., Ltd., *Singapore*
Prentice-Hall, Inc., *Englewood Cliffs, New Jersey*

Text set in 10/11 pt IBM Press Roman, printed by photolithography, and bound in Great Britain at The Pitman Press, Bath

79 80 81 82 83   7 6 5 4 3

Contents

v

Preface

There are a number of good books which deal with the mechanics of double-entry book-keeping; but in general they fail to give sufficient emphasis to the assumptions underlying the traditional historical cost model within which context double-entry book-keeping is introduced. On the other hand, the more academic textbooks tend to dismiss double-entry book-keeping as a 'mere technique' which can be easily learned. We agree that it can be easily learned, if it is properly taught. However, it is clear that the new generation of students who are introduced to accounting in the class room rather than in the field, often find difficulty in mastering this important 'mere technique'. This difficulty means that they experience quite unnecessary problems during their more advanced accounting studies. We have written this book, therefore, because we could not find an existing textbook which fulfilled the two aims of our introductory teaching. The aims are, first to give a clear understanding of historical cost accounting and, secondly, to provide students with a grounding in double-entry book-keeping.

We believe that one of the problems of learning accounting is that students are often too quickly rushed on to such topics as partnerships or manufacturing accounts when they still do not know whether they are on their debit or their credit. So we have confined this text to a consideration of a simple, sole trading retailer. We have cheated from time to time by introducing more complex situations when discussing such matters as depreciation. We will make our more leisurely progress to the problems of accounting for other forms of business entities in the second volume.

There are two features of this book which we hope will make it especially useful to accounting novices. One is our concentration on accrual accounting which is such an important feature of the traditional accounting model. The other is the introduction, in Chapter 10, of the work sheet approach to the preparation of accounting statements. We feel that this is a useful approach, not only because of its practical implications, but also because of the further emphasis it places on the duality aspect of the double-entry method.

This book is primarily designed for the first term or so of a Foundation Course or a degree course. It should also be of interest to managers and other users of financial statements, because of the stress we have placed on providing our readers with an understanding of the nature of the statements and of the items contained therein.

The material on which this book is based has been used by students at the City of London Polytechnic for the past couple of years. We are grateful to our colleagues for their helpful suggestions which enabled us to incorporate a number of improvements. The mistakes that remain are, of course, very much our own. This book seems to have been through innumerable drafts and we are most grateful to Mesdames Gambie, Reeves and Cooper for their efforts at their various typewriters. But most of all we want to thank our students, without whom there would be no book.

We would also like to thank Ronald Decent and Alfred Waller of Prentice-Hall International, our publishers, for their help and encouragement. Professor Peter Bird of the University of Kent at Canterbury has read the manuscript on behalf of our publishers and we are grateful for the improvements he has suggested.

R.W.L.
I.D.G.

1 | *What is Accounting?*

Accounting contains elements both of science and art. The important thing is that it is not merely a collection of arithmetical techniques but a set of complex processes depending on and prepared for people. The human aspect, which many people, especially accountants, forget, arises because:

1. most accounting reports of any significance depend, to a greater or lesser extent, on people's opinions and estimates;
2. accounting reports are prepared in order to help people make decisions;
3. accounting reports are based on activities which have been carried out by people.

But what specifically is accounting? It is very difficult to find a pithy definition that is all-inclusive but we can say that accounting is concerned with:

the provision of information in financial terms that will help in decisions concerning resource allocation, and the preparation of reports in financial terms describing the effects of past resource allocation decisions.

Examples of resource allocation decisions are:

Should an investor buy or sell shares?
Should a bank manager lend money to a firm?
How much tax should a company pay?
Which collective farm should get the extra tractor?

As you can see, accounting is needed in any society requiring resource allocation and its usefulness is not confined to 'capitalist' or 'mixed' economies.

An accountant is concerned with the provision and interpretation of financial information. He does not, as an accountant, make decisions. Many accountants do of course get directly involved in decision making but when they do they are wearing a different hat.

Accounting is also concerned with reporting on the effects of past decisions. But one should consider whether this is done for its own sake or whether it is done in order to provide information which it is hoped will prove helpful in current and future decisions. We contend that knowledge of the past is relevant only if it can be used to help in making current and future decisions, for we can hope that we shall be able to influence the future by making appropriate decisions but we cannot redo the past . Thus the measurement of past results is a subsidiary role, but because of the historical development of accounting and, perhaps, because of the limitations of the present state of the art, 'backward looking' accounting sometimes appears to be an end in itself and not as a means that will help in achieving a more fundamental objective.

PLANNING AND CONTROL

We may describe the making of current decisions as *planning* and should consider how the reporting of past activities can help in the planning process. A knowledge of the past might help in the estimation of future outcomes. For example, a manager wishing to estimate the costs of manufacturing a new product would find it helpful to know the cost of manufacturing similar products in the past.

Another aspect of measuring the past is *control.* Here past results are compared with some targets or standard, and knowledge of the difference between the actual and target may be used in various ways to improve future performance.

1. If past results are not as good as expected then (assuming the expectations are reasonable) remedial action needs to be taken and this will give rise to a current, planning, decision.
2. The difference between actual and target results may suggest that there errors have been made in past decisions, and this knowledge can serve to refine the planning process.

Thus planning and control are very clearly linked; indeed it could be argued that they are indivisible.

FINANCIAL AND MANAGEMENT ACCOUNTING

A distinction is often made between *financial* and *management* accounting. Financial accounting consists basically of the preparation of financial statements which cover the whole of the activities of a business, charity, golf club, etc. (or, to start using jargon, an *entity*) and which are primarily intended for use by people outside the entity. Management accounting, on the other hand, tends to be concerned with parts of the entity as well as the whole, and is intended to help decision making by those who are inside the firm.

However, too much can be made of this distinction, for the same basic information is used for both financial and management accounting, and both insiders and outsiders have to make decisions which are of the same fundamental nature.

Past Financial Accounting

In this introductory book we shall be concerned with financial accounting, concentrating on the reporting of past activities. We shall also confine our attention to one of the simpler forms of business entity — the sole trader.

Financial accounting may be seen as consisting of:

Recording
Classification
Presentation
Interpretation

of financial information.

The recording stage and most of the classification stage is fairly routine and is usually called book-keeping (which can be pretty boring once you have learnt it) to distinguish it from the interesting, and lucrative, work of the accountant. However, life being what it is, you have to master book-keeping if you are really to understand accounting. In order to understand the sort of information that is recorded, classified, and presented, it will be useful to consider the immediate aim of the financial accounting process. This is the preparation of balance sheets and income statements. These will be discussed fully in later chapters but it is convenient for us to sketch the main features of a balance sheet at this stage.

A balance sheet is a statement of assets (things owned by an entity) and liabilities (things owed by an entity) at a point in time, with the difference between the assets and liabilities being known as owners' equity. The difference between owners' equity at the start and the end of a period gives the profit for the period (if we assume that the owners do not introduce additional resources or withdraw any resources).

CONVENTIONS

An important point that must be grasped at the outset is that a balance sheet is not a statement showing the current economic values of the assets nor the current economic value of the business as a whole. To see what bases are used in balance sheets (and income statements) it is necessary to study accounting conventions or, as they are sometimes misleadingly called, principles. These conventions may be viewed as the rules of the game, but rules which are sometimes broken for the most respectable of reasons by the most respectable of accountants. Many writers have suggested various lists of conventions underlying current practice; but the following is a list that would command wide acceptance and will help you understand the chapters that follow.

Objectivity.   Accountants seek to prepare accounting statements that are as free as possible from personal opinion or bias, i.e. that are not subjective. An important extension of this is that assets are recorded at their original acquisition cost, or *historical cost*, rather than at their current values.

Verifiability.   So far as possible, figures used in accounting statements should be capable of independent verification. Verifiability has been defined by the American Accounting Association as 'that attribute of information which allows qualified individuals working independently of one another to develop essentially similar measures or conclusions from an examination of the same evidence, data or records'. It can be seen that objectivity and verifiability are essentially allied concepts.

Consistency.   We shall show that there are numerous instances where an entity can choose between different accounting methods. In general, the entity should adopt a consistent approach to like items.

Relevance.   Data that are relevant to the purpose in hand should be presented and only those data. This convention is more relevant in management accounting than in financial accounting, since, in the former, reports tend to be prepared for special purposes while, by the nature of the latter, financial accounting statements are prepared for outsiders who will want to use them for a variety of purposes.

Stable Money Unit.   It is assumed that money is a stable measuring unit, i.e. that pounds of different periods can be added in the same way as last year's metres can be added to this year's metres. In the United Kingdom some firms publish supplementary accounting statements which are not based on this assumption, but it is still maintained in the preparation of the basic accounting statements.

Duality.   Accounting regards every transaction as having two aspects. For example, if a business buys machinery for cash, the asset 'machinery' is increased and the asset 'cash' is decreased. We do not take the view that cash is 'converted' directly into machinery, which could be said to have only one aspect. The specific technique which reflects the concept of duality is known as *double-entry* book-keeping, which will be discussed in the following chapters.

Conservatism. Faced with a choice, accountants will usually take the gloomy view, showing the lowest reasonable figure of current profit; they will always ensure that all losses are recorded in respect of any period but will not take account of any profit which is not certain. The reasons for this are in part historical, arising, for example, from the need not to mislead creditors into oversetimating the credit-worthiness of a firm. However, the damage and limitations arising from conservatism are, nowadays, increasingly being recognized.

Materiality. The accountant will not necessarily take special notice of a given item if it is not material in the context of the firm, its business and its size, e.g. an item of an unusual nature which would normally require separate display may be included as part of sundry expenses if the amount involved is insignificant compared to the overall size of the undertaking.

The above rules are often in conflict with each other, relevance and objectivity in particular, and some of the rules may be considered to be inappropriate in certain circumstances. For example, firms engaged in long-term contracts often depart from a strict reliance on the historical cost convention.

It must not be thought that the conventions came first with accounting practice being based on them. On the contrary, these conventions may be thought of as being a rationalization of what accountants actually do. The situation has been likened to the painting of road signs stating the speed limits. The equivalent road sign to accounting conventions would be prepared by someone who has watched the traffic in a built-up area for a while and eventually paints a sign saying 'speed limit about 37 miles per hour or, sometimes, 60'.

EXERCISES

1.1 Jake, a gentleman farmer, used to employ a farm manager but having seen the financial results for a period Jake sacked the manager.

Assuming that Jake is rational, say in what ways his action exhibits planning and control.

1.2 Jack and Jill have a new pail (which cost £5) and £3 in cash. Their other assets, such as they are, can be ignored. They estimate that their pail will be capable of surviving 10,000 journeys to the well.

Jack and Jill went up the hill and found that they had to pay £2 to fill their pail with water.

On the way down Jack fell and broke a passer-by's spectacles. Jack promised to pay for the damage and the myopic stranger said he thought that his spectacles could be repaired for between £4 and £6.

At the bottom of the hill (a long one) Jack and Jill found someone who paid them £10 for half the water in their pail. Other potential customers are fast approaching and a rumour has started that the fellow at the top of the hill is now charging £3 for a pailful. Since Jack and Jill started their journey the price of pails has doubled.

List Jack and Jill's assets and liabilities at this time and hence say how much better (or worse) off they are since they started their journey. In doing so, use whatever accounting conventions seem appropriate and indicate which ones you have used.

2 | Balance Sheets and Income Statements

BALANCE SHEETS

One feature of an accountant's work that may impress the uninitiated is his
ability to produce a balance sheet that balances, i.e. a mass of seemingly un-
intelligible figures are skilfully arranged into two columns so that the totals
of the columns are exactly equal. We fear that we shall have to shatter any
image you may have of the accountant as some white-coated scientific
worker carefully weighing out figures until his finely adjusted balance comes
quivering to rest in the equilibrium position. The whole thing is a bit of a
confidence trick really because:

> A balance sheet balances because, by definition, it must.
> Why?
> A balance sheet is a list of the assets owned by the entity (one
> column) and a statement indicating the sources of the assets (the
> other column).

Since assets do not appear out of the air* each asset has a source and thus
the balancing of the balance sheet is ensured.

$$A \equiv L + E$$

This statement is sometimes rather grandiloquently called 'The Fundamental Accounting Equation'† and simply repeats the above observation
that the assets (A) must equal the sources $(L + E)$.

---

* Even if they did we could still produce a balance sheet,

	Assets		*Sources*	
Cash	£100		Out of the air	£100

† This is an identity rather than an equation as it holds for all values of A, L and
E; so we shall use the identity sign ($\equiv$) rather than the equality sign.

An entity can obtain its assets from two sources, the owners or outsiders. The owners' source is known as the *owners' equity* or sometimes just equity (*E*) while the outsiders' source is called the *liabilities* (*L*). Of course the outsiders do not provide assets for nothing; they will expect to be repaid in cash or in kind.

The balance sheet will not indicate the actual source of a specific asset; what it does show is a pool of assets and a pool of sources. There can be movements within each pool, i.e. one form of asset can be exchanged for another or one form of source can replace another. There can also be transfers of assets to sources. If a liability is paid off, we reduce the total assets and at the same time reduce the 'outsiders' source'. The sorts of movements that one can find will be shown shortly, but first it will be useful to learn something about the way that financial statements are prepared for sole traders.

THE TRANSACTIONS OF A SOLE TRADER

So that you can follow the examples it is necessary for us to introduce some definitions and explain some of the problems involved in accounting for sole traders.

1. A sole trader may be defined as an individual carrying on a business with a view to profit, with no other person sharing in the ownership of the business.
2. The business should be kept separate from the individual. Even though the law does not recognize the business of a sole trader as being a distinct legal entity (as it does for limited companies) accountants do attempt to produce accounting statements which relate solely to the business and do not include 'private' assets and liabilities.
3. The resources provided by the owner are known as capital and the resources withdrawn by the owner as drawings.

We shall now examine some of the transactions of a sole trader. Note how, at all times, the identity $A \equiv L + E$ is maintained. In the analysis sheet (Figure 2.1) you will see that cumulative columns are provided for *A*, *L* and *E* and the figures in these columns at any point in time will give the balance sheet totals; however, a certain amount of analysis is required in order to provide the detailed balance sheet.

1. Mack started a business dealing in bits on 1 January 19X5 with cash of £1,000; he paid this into a newly opened bank account which he considered to be his business bank account.
2. He purchased some bits for £300 for cash on 2 January 19X5.

3. On 3 January 19X5 he purchased some more bits, for £400, but this time his supplier, Jones, allowed him credit.
4. Mack decided that in order to sell his bits he would need a car. He already owned a car, and he decided that as from 4 January 19X5 this car should be treated as an asset of the business instead of being considered a private asset. It would cost about £200 of purchase a car of the same model and condition as Mack's.
5. On 6 January 19X5 Mack paid Jones £200.
6. The original capital contribution of £1,000 had left Mack a bit short of cash so he took £100 out of his business bank account for his living expenses.
7. Mack decided that he would need more cash in order to run his business and so approached his friend Smith and asked for a loan. Much to Mack's, and our, surprise Smith agreed and said that he would give Mack £500 in cash and would himself pay Jones, Mack's bits supplier, £100. This he did on 7 January 19X5.

These events are recorded in Figure 2.1. We can see that as at the close of business on 7 January the identity is satisfied, i.e.

$$A \equiv L + E$$
$$£1,800 \equiv £700 + £1,100$$

These figures are merely the balance sheet totals but with a bit of analysis we can prepare a balance sheet:

MACK
Balance Sheet as at 7 January 19X5

Assets	£	£	
Car		200	
Inventory		700	
Cash		900	
		£1,800	

Financed by:

Liabilities

Trade creditor (Jones)	100		
Loan (Smith)	600		
		700	
Owners' equity		1,100	
		£1,800	

Figure 2.1 Transactions Analysis Sheet

	Date	Assets (A) +	−	Cumulative	Liabilities (L) +	−	Cumulative	Equity (E) +	−	Cumulative	L + E Cumulative
1	Jan 1	1,000 (Cash)		1,000				1,000 (Capital)		1,000	1,000
2	2	300 (Inventory)	300 (Cash)	1,000						1,000	1,000
3	3	400 (Inventory)		1,400	400 (Jones)		400			1,000	1,400
4	4	200 (Car)		1,600			400	200 (Capital)		1,200	1,600
5	5		200 (Cash)	1,400		200 (Jones)	200			1,200	1,400
6	6		100 (Cash)	1,300			200		100 (Drawings)	1,100	1,300
7(i)	7	500 (Cash)		1,800	500 (Smith)		700			1,100	1,800
7(ii)	7			1,800	100 (Smith)	100 (Jones)	700			1,100	1,800

Comments   At all times $A \equiv L + E$. There are nine ways in which the identity can be manipulated. These are:

	Item in Figure 2.1
Increase asset and decrease asset	(2)
and increase liability	(3)
and increase equity	(1)
Decrease asset and decrease liability	(5)
and decrease equity	(6)
Increase liability and decrease liability	(7ii)
and decrease equity	(a)
Decrease liability and increase equity	(b)
Increase equity and decrease equity	(c)

The above does not illustrate (a), (b) and (c). An example of (a) would be the business taking over a 'private' liability of Mack's, while (b) could be the reverse, i.e. Mack himself taking over a liability of the business. Since with a sole trader no attempt is made to distinguish between different sorts of owners' equity, it is not possible to think of an example of (c) in this context. However, such a transaction would be relevant in the case of a limited company, where it is meaningful to talk about different forms of owners' equity.

We have introduced the word *inventory* which may not be familiar to all our readers. This is an American term meaning 'stock of goods for resale' and is probably a better word to use than the British 'stock' as this can be confused with other forms of stock (as in 'stocks and shares').

Notice that the balance sheet has been stated as being 'as at 7 January 19X5', since a balance sheet is a statement of assets and their sources at a particular point in time.

ASSETS

We have thrown the word *asset* about with some abandon, and we should now attempt to explain more precisely what we mean by the term.

An asset is any right which is of economic value to its owner. The right may be a general one; for example, the ownership of cash allows the owner to exercise a general power to command resources. On the other hand it may be highly specific, such as a prepaid insurance premium, which gives the owner the benefit of being insured for the period covered by the payment.

This is a good enough general definition of an asset, but because of

the accounting conventions outlined in Chapter 1 we need to be more
restrictive when deciding whether to recognize an asset for inclusion in the
accounting records.

The conditions we need to apply are:

1. The asset must be acquired for a measurable cost. This is necessary
   if we are to satisfy the historical cost convention.
2. It must be owned by the business (a sole proprietorship, not being
   a legal entity, cannot own assets; so in these cases the assets must
   belong to the proprietor and be held for use in the business).
3. The asset must be capable of yielding future economic benefits.
   There are two points here:

   (a) The asset must still be of some use, in that it will produce
   benefits in the future. This may seem obvious, but in practice one
   does occasionally come across items which are still shown as assets
   but which are worthless.

   (b) The benefits must be of an economic, or pecuniary, nature
   such that the cash flow to the business would be reduced in the
   future if the business were deprived of the use of the asset without
   compensation. Possessions which delight the eye but which could
   not yield extra cash do not qualify as assets for our purpose.

We shall return to the question of assets and their relationship with
expenses in Chapter 5.

LIABILITIES

We have already identified liabilities as the 'asset source' from outsiders.

In the above example we differentiated between two sorts of liabilities: trade creditors (or just creditors), the source resulting from suppliers
providing goods or services before they are paid for them, and loans where
(in general) cash is provided by the outsider in exchange for a promise that
the cash will be repaid (with interest) in the future. Trade credit, which is
practically always interest free, lasts for a comparatively short time (although
it is continually being renewed) while loans may be for any length of time,
depending on the agreement between the borrower and lender.

Another important type of liability is a business's obligation to provide a service. For example, a magazine that receives subscriptions in advance
has, until the period of the subscription expires, an obligation to provide
the subscriber with the magazine.

A liability may be recognized even if the actual sum involved cannot
be determined with any accuracy. For example, a business might offer a
guarantee when selling goods and although it may only be able to make a
very rough estimate of the costs that it will have to incur in carrying out
its obligation, it should still recognize the liability. The word 'provision' is

used to describe this type of liability whose existence is known, although the amount cannot be determined with a reasonable degree of accuracy.

THE INCOME STATEMENT

Mack is not going to get rich playing around with his assets, liabilities and equity; he had better get on with some trading.

Let us suppose that on 8 January 19X5 he sold, for £150 cash, bits which originally cost him £100. We shall now consider in detail the effect of that transaction.

Assets, in total, have been increased by £50, the asset cash having been increased by £150 and the asset inventory decreased by £100. What is the source of this increase in assets? The source is the owner. Through trading, the business has made a profit; the owner could have withdrawn that profit, but as he has not done so he has allowed the business to increase its assets by £50.

It is better to think of the transaction as being split into two parts as follows:

$$A \quad \equiv \quad L \quad + \quad E$$
$$+£150 \qquad\qquad +£150$$
$$\text{(cash)} \qquad \text{(revenue; sales)}$$

and

$$A \quad \equiv \quad L \quad + \quad E$$
$$-£100 \qquad\qquad -£100$$
$$\text{(inventory)} \quad \text{(expenses; cost of goods sold)}$$

The receipt of the £150 is known as the revenue, and the £100 that was used up in earning that revenue, as an expense. A more rigorous discussion of revenue and expenses is given in Chapter 5. Revenue and expenses are part of owners' equity, but it is convenient to keep them separate from the rest of owners' equity and from each other, at least for a while.

If Mack had sold the goods on credit instead of for cash there would be no significant difference, for instead of having an increase in cash he would have a new asset, debtors.

The Mack saga is continued below and this time we have extended the analysis sheet (Figure 2.2) to include columns for revenue and expenses. Remember, however, that they are part of equity, revenue increasing equity and expenses decreasing equity.

1. The interest on the loan is £1 a day but, at the time of writing, nothing has been paid to Smith.
2. On 8 January Mack sold, for £150 cash, goods which cost him £100.

Figure 2.2 Transactions Analysis Sheet

	Date	Assets (A) +	Assets (A) −	Assets Cumul-ative	Liabilities (L) +	Liabilities (L) −	Liabilities Cumul-ative	Capital subscribed and withdrawn (E') +	Capital subscribed and withdrawn (E') −	E' Cumul-ative	Revenue (R)	Expenses (X)	R−X Cumul-ative	E = E'+R−X Cumul-ative	L+E Cumul-ative
	Jan 8			1,800			700			1,100				1,100	1,800
1	8			1,800	1 (Interest payable)		701			1,100		1 (Interest)	−1	1,099	1,800
2(a)	8	150 (Cash)		1,950			701			1,100	150 (Sales)		149	1,249	1,950
2(b)	8		100 (Inventory)	1,850			701			1,100		100 (Cost of goods sold)	49	1,149	1,850
1	9			1,850	1 (Interest payable)		702			1,100		1 (Interest)	48	1,148	1,850
3	9	250 (Inventory)		2,100	250 (Tree)		952			1,100			48	1,148	2,100
1	10			2,100	1 (Interest payable)		953			1,100		1 (Interest)	47	1,147	2,100
4(a)	10	300 (Rolt)		2,400			953			1,100	300 (Sales)		347	1,447	2,400

Ref	No.		Detail				Detail			
4(b)	10		200 (Inventory)	2,200	953	1,100	200 (Cost of goods sold)	147	1,247	2,200
1	11			2,200	954 / 1 (Interest payable)	1,100	1 (Interest)	146	1,246	2,200
5	11	300 (Prepaid rent)	300 (Cash)	2,200	954	1,100		146	1,246	2,200
1	12			2,200	955 / 1 (Interest payable)	1,100	1 (Interest)	145	1,245	2,200
5	12		10 (Prepaid rent)	2,190	955	1,100	10 (Rent)	135	1,235	2,190
1	13			2,190	956 / 1 (Interest payable)	1,100	1 (Interest)	134	1,234	2,190
5	13		10 (Prepaid rent)	2,180	956	1,100	10 (Rent)	124	1,224	2,180
6	13		5 (Cash)	2,175	956	1,100	5 (Petrol)	119	1,219	2,175
7	13		6 (Cash)	2,169	956	1,100	6 (Wages)	113	1,213	2,169
8	13		50 (Cash)	2,119	956	50 / 1,050		113	1,163	2,119

3. On 9 January Mack purchased more bits on credit from Tree for £250.
4. On 10 January Mack sold, for £300, some bits to Rolt on credit; they had cost him £200.
5. On 11 January Mack paid £300 rental in advance for a shop for the period commencing on 12 January. The rental is £10 per day.
6. Mack purchased petrol for the car belonging to the business for £5 on 13 January.
7. On the same day he started to employ an assistant Ted, to whom he paid £6 a day. Ted was paid at the end of each day.
8. On 13 January Mack withdrew £50 to pay for his living expenses.

As before, we can see the outline of the balance sheet, as at 13 January 19X5.

	£	£
Assets		2,119
Liabilities	956	
Owners' equity	1,163	
		2,119

By analysing Figures 2.1 and 2.2 we can find the details.

Mack's balance sheet is given below but, at the moment, we want to concentrate on the change in owners' equity.

	£
Owners' equity, 8 January 19X5	1,100
add Revenue less expenses	
for the period	113
	1,213
less Drawings	50
Owners' equity 13 January 19X5	£1,163

We can see that £113 represents that part of the change in owners' equity due to the trading operations for the period. The function of the income statement (or profit and loss account) is to explain the composition of this figure. The income statement in contrast to the balance sheet, covers a period of time and this should always be shown in its heading.

Given all that and with a good deal of scribbling to find out the cash balance, etc. we are now in a position to produce Mack's financial statements.

MACK
Income Statement for the period 8–13, January 19X5

	£	£
Sales		450
less Cost of goods sold	300	
Interest	6	
Rent	20	
Petrol	5	
Wages	6	337
Profit for the period		£113

Balance Sheet as at 13 January 19X5

Assets	£	£
Car		200
Inventory		650
Trade debtors (Rolt)		300
Prepaid rent		280
Cash		689
		£2,119

Financed by:

Liabilities

Trade creditors (Jones & Tree)	350	
Interest payable	6	
Loan (Smith)	600	956

Owners' equity

Capital at 8 January 19X5	1,100	
add Profit for the period	113	
	1,213	
less Drawings	50	1,163
		£2,119

Comments   The treatment of the interest deserves some explanation. Mack (in the guise of his business) has agreed to pay interest on the loan, which works out (conveniently for us) at £1 a day. Interest is an expense of running the business, and as it has not been paid it represents a liability. However, we can still interpret it in terms of assets and sources in that the lender, having not been paid his interest, is providing assets. So we have the same pool of assets, but each day £1 is transferred from the equity source to the liabilities source.

The treatment of interest in the work sheet is correct*, if tedious, but a short cut is permissible. The transfer could have been done all at once on 13 January, replacing all the individual entries by one:

$$A \equiv L \ + \ E$$

$$+£6 \quad -£6$$

A similar short cut could have been used for rent. This short cut is helpful when doing the exercise at the end of this chapter but you should realize that its use means that the affairs of the business are not being recorded in a strictly correct fashion, since the cumulative totals will not give the balance sheet totals until the omnibus entry is made.

Mack purchased some petrol on 13 January for £5. It is probable that some petrol was left in the tank at the end of the day, and also possible that some was used on private journeys. If these assumptions are correct, we should show an asset at 13 January and record the petrol used for non-business purposes as drawings. The effect of both of these would be to reduce the petrol expense. However, the amounts involved would be small and the convention of materiality would be invoked to justify our doing nothing about them.

Any amount taken out of the business by its owner is described as drawings and is not included in the income statement. This is true even if the owner works in the business and describes, and considers, the amounts withdrawn as his wages. This practice is in some ways an unfortunate one, since without a charge for the owner's time (which is often the most significant item) the expenses of earning revenue are understated. The reason the practice is adopted is that there is no reason to suppose that the amount withdrawn by the owner is anything like the amount that would have to be paid to a manager to do the work. This amount can be estimated, but this estimate would not be considered to be sufficiently objective for inclusion in the financial statements.

If you look at the owners' equity section of Mack's balance sheet you will see that there are a number of items. The actual balance sheet figure is £1,163 but it is the practice to show how the balance of owners' equity reconciles with the opening owners' equity, i.e. that shown on the last balance sheet.

CONCLUSION

In this section we have introduced you to the balance sheet (a list of assets and their sources at a point of time) and the income statement (a state-

---

*Actually the transfer from equity to liabilities is a continuous one so even our day-by-day transfer is not strictly correct but we have to draw the line somewhere.

ment explaining the change in owners' equity due to the trading operations of the business). We have also shown a systematic but cumbersome method of deriving these statements. Clearly our method will not be of much use for dealing with any but the smallest business, but do not fear: much of the rest of this book is concerned with a description of more practical methods of recording financial transactions and deriving balance sheets and income statements.

EXERCISES

2.1 You are given the following information, all of which relates to 31 December 19X6, in respect of Nina's Dress Shop.

	£
Inventory	900
Creditors	600
Delivery van	1,000
Wages due	50
Debtors	100
Nina's capital account	1,630
Prepaid rent	80
Cash	?

Prepare Nina's balance sheet at 31 December 19X6.

2.2 From the following information find x.

	£
Assets at 31 December 19X6	7,000
Loss for the year ended 31 December 19X6	2,000
Owner's equity at 1 January 19X6	6,000
Capital introduced during the year ended 31 December 19X6	1,000
Capital withdrawn during the year ended 31 December 19X6	3,000
Liabilities at 31 December 19X6	x

2.3 You are the owner of a small shop dealing in tobacco, confectionery and newspapers, etc.

Required:

For each of the following events:

(a) state whether you believe that the event has improved the prospects of your business, i.e. do you believe that the event would increase the sum, albeit by a small amount, you would receive if you sold the business?

and

(b) where appropriate analyse the events in terms of the assets, liabilities and equity of your business. Use an analysis sheet of the form used in Figure 2.2 in the text.

Treat each part of the question independently

1. You purchase, on credit, 10 cases of chocolate bars for £100.

2. You pay rates of £200 for 6 months in advance.

3. You sell goods which cost you £30 for £40, half for cash and half on credit.

4. You receive a legacy of £1,000 which you pay into your business bank account.

5. You purchase a delivery van for £800 cash.

6. You purchase 10 reels of typewriter ribbon for £5 cash. One reel is put into your typewriter while the others are included in inventory.

7. The local bus company has moved a bus stop to just outside your shop; it had previously been 100 yards away.

8. The manufacturer of Smock's biscuits announces that the trade price of the biscuits is increased from 8 pence to 10 pence per packet and that the recommended selling price is now 14 pence instead of 12 pence per packet. You have in inventory 500 packets purchased at 8 pence per packet.

9. The manufacturer of Ray's All Sorts announces that the trade price is reduced from 16 pence to 12 pence per packet and that the recommended selling price is now 14 pence instead of 18 pence per packet. You have in inventory 1,000 packets which cost you 16 pence per packet.

10. The off licence opposite has diversified its activities and has started to sell confectionery.

2.4 Bourne and Masons is a large department store employing some 900 staff. During the last few months of 19X8 the store's management decided that they should send a number of the staff on training programmes. The courses covered general matters but were also geared to the particular jobs currently being done by the staff. The courses cost about £10,000.

Discuss whether or not the expenditure has resulted in the creation of a 'business asset' as at 31 December 19X8.

2.5 Clive started business as a seller of widgets on day 1 by transferring £5,000 from his private bank account to a newly opened business bank account.

From the start he employed an assistant, Steve. Clive agreed to pay him £3 per day, the payments being made every 3 days, i.e. days 3, 6, 9, etc.

Clive's other transactions for the period day 1 to day 10 were as follows:

1. Day 1 Acquired, for cash, the lease of a shop for £2,000.

2. Day 1 Acquired, on credit from XP Limited, fixtures and fittings for the shop, amounting to £1,000.

3. Day 1 Acquired, on credit from SA Limited, 50 widgets for £8 each.

4. Day 1 Acquired, for cash, 12 widgets at £7 each. Clive also paid £12 for the carriage of these goods to his shop.

5. Day 2 Sold, on credit to CA, 4 widgets for £12 each.

6. Day 3 Sold, on credit to CB, 6 widgets for £12 each.

7. Day 3 Purchased, on credit from SB Limited, 10 widgets at £10 each.

8. Day 4 Clive agreed that two of the widgets sold to CA were defective and they were returned to him. One of them was repaired by Steve. This required the purchase (for cash) of sundry materials of £2. The repaired widget was retained in stock. The other widget was returned to the original supplier, SA Limited.

9. Day 5 Sold, for cash, 10 widgets for £14 each.

10. Day 6 Sold, on credit to CC, 20 widgets. The selling price was £14 each but as CC is Clive's wife's cousin, Clive agreed that CC could have a discount of 10%.

11. Day 7 Received £50 from CB on account.

12. Day 7 Received from CA the total amount due from him.

13. Day 9 Sold, for cash, 4 widgets at £15 each.

14. Day 10 Clive withdrew £20 for his own use.

15. Day 10 Paid XP Limited £500 and SB Limited the whole amount due.

Clive's sundry expenses, which are outstanding at the end of Day 10, are £5 per day.

Assume that the widgets are sold in the order in which they were acquired. (This is known as the 'First in First Out' method).

Required:

(a) Complete the analysis sheet (as used in Figure 2.2 in the text) recording the above transactions.

(b) Prepare Clive's balance sheet as at day 10 and his income statement for the period day 1 to day 10.

(You may use the short cut referred to in the text).

3 | Debit and Credit; T Accounts

Those who suffered their way through the last exercise in Chapter 2 will not require convincing of the need for a more systematic approach to the maintenance of accounting records.

The practice of book-keeping is an ancient one which has developed over the centuries. One interesting feature of its history is that, unlike many other skills or trades, the most important single development to date did not take place in the Industrial Revolution of the last century or during the Transistor Revolution of the last few decades but occurred in Renaissance Europe (almost certainly in Italy). This development was the recognition of the duality convention discussed in Chapter 1, or in other words the invention of *double-entry book-keeping.*

In order to understand the workings of this method it is necessary to introduce the language of accounting and, in particular, the key words *debit* and *credit.*

The meaning of these words will be understood if we reintroduce the accounting identity, i.e.

$$A \quad \equiv \quad L \quad + \quad E$$
$$\text{(Assets)} \quad \text{(Liabilities)} \quad \text{(Owners' equity)}$$

Every transaction has two effects on the above identity, with the effects being such that the equality of the identity is maintained at all times. So, for example, if a transaction reduces an asset it must also:

increase another asset, or
decrease a liability, or
decrease owners' equity.

More generally, if one effect of the transaction is to reduce the left-hand side of the identity then the other effect must be either to increase the left-hand side or decrease the right-hand side by the same amount.

In fact every transaction can be broken down into two components, one that:

increases the left-hand side, or
decreases the right-hand side

and one that:

decreases the left-hand side, or
increases the right-hand side.

The first group is the debit part of the transaction while the second group is the credit component.

The above is merely a definitional statement but we can go further. Since the accounting identity is an identity it must be satisfied at all times. Thus for any transaction, the debit must equal the credit. Diagrammatically the position can be represented as follows:

↑Debit		↑Credit
A	≡	$\overbrace{L + E}$
↓Credit		↓Debit

Example 3.1

1. Jack pays £1,000 in cash to acquire a new car.

Debit	£1,000	increase assets (car)
Credit	£1,000	decrease assets (cash)

$$\begin{array}{ccc} ↑£1,000 & & \\ A & ≡ & L + E \\ ↓£1,000 & & \end{array}$$

2. Jack obtains the above car on credit.

Debit	£1,000	increase assets (car)
Credit	£1,000	increase liabilities (sundry creditor)

$$\begin{array}{ccccc} ↑£1,000 & & ↑£1,000 & & \\ A & ≡ & L & + & E \end{array}$$

3 Jack withdraws £30 from his business bank account to pay his living expenses.

Debit	£30	decrease owners' equity (drawings)
Credit	£30	decrease assets (cash)

$$\begin{array}{ccccc} A & ≡ & L + E & & \\ ↓£30 & & L & + & E \\ & & & & ↓£30 \end{array}$$

4. Jack borrows £500 from his grandmother who also pays off one of Jack's trade creditors to whom he owed £100.

Debit	£500	increase assets (cash)
Debit	£100	decrease liabilities (trade creditors)
Credit	£600	increase liabilities (loan)

$$\uparrow £500 \qquad\qquad \uparrow £600$$

$$A \qquad \equiv \qquad L \quad + \quad E$$

$$\downarrow £100$$

Note that in Example 3.1.4 there are two debits but the essential point remains: the total of the debits equals the total of the credits. We could have treated it as two transactions, (1) the provision of cash, and (2) paying off the creditor. That would have been long-winded; so it is usual to record such events in the way shown.

THE EXTENDED ACCOUNTING IDENTITY

We have not so far in this chapter discussed changes in owners' equity that occur due to the trading operations of the business. To include these we shall extend the accounting identity to incorporate revenue and expenses.

Let R = Revenue
      X = Expenses
      P = Profit, i.e. $R - X$.

Let us consider a period in time. At the start of the period $A \equiv L + E$, but as we want to focus on the changes in owners' equity that result from trading operations we shall replace E by E' where E' is defined as:

owners' equity at the start of the period + additional capital subscribed − capital withdrawn other than through the trading operations of the business.

Successful trading results in a profit which is an increase in owners' equity and, as we showed in Chapter 2, this will also result in an increase in assets and/or a decrease in liabilities.

So for any point in time during the period we can say:

$$A \equiv L + E' + P.$$

Substituting

$$R - X \equiv P$$

$$A \equiv L + E' + R - X$$

or rearranging

$$A + X \equiv L + E' + R$$

and as before,

> Debits cause an increase in the left-hand side or a decrease in the right-hand side

while

> Credits cause a decrease in the left-hand side or an increase in the right-hand side.

That is:

↑Debit		↑Credit
$A + X$	$\equiv$	$L + E' + R$
↓Credit		↓Debit

So an increase in assets and an increase in expenses are both called debits*.

In deciding whether a transaction gives rise to an asset or an expense, reference must be made to the period under consideration. For example, consider the payment of insurance of £1,200 made on 31 March 19X4 for the year 1 April 19X4 to 31 March 19X5. If the accounting period under review were the year ended 31 March 19X4, the transaction would result in the creation of an asset, prepaid insurance, of £1,200. However, if the period were the year ended 30 June 19X4, then we have both an expense, insurance of £300 (covering the period 1 April 19X4 to 30 June 19X4) and and asset, prepaid insurance of £900. We shall return to this point later.

Losses

Even if the trading operations are unprofitable, the extended identity remains unchanged.

Let $L' \equiv$ Loss, i.e. $X - R$

Then
$$A \equiv L + E' - L'$$
$$A \equiv L + E' - (X - R)$$
$$A \equiv L + E' - X + R$$
$$A + X \equiv L + E' + R$$

and this is the extended accounting identity that we derived above.

* The habit of many speakers and writers of drawing on accounting for their metaphors can lead to some confusion. When referring to the unfavourable aspects of an affair they will say 'on the debit side'. But a debit can refer to an increase in assets, which is pleasant, as well as an increase in expenses, which is presumably unpleasant. It is better to stick to cricket as a source of metaphors.

Example 3.2

In this example it will be assumed that the period under review is the year ended 31 December 19X5.

1. Fred sells goods on credit for £500. The goods had originally cost him £350.

   Debit   £500   increase assets (trade debtors)
   Credit £500   increase revenue (sales)
   Debit   £350   increase expenses (cost of goods sold)
   Credit £350   decrease assets (inventory)

   ↑£500   ↑£350   ↑£500

   $$A \quad + \quad X \quad \equiv \quad L + E' + R$$

   ↓£350

2. Fred pays an insurance premium of £100 on 25 May 19X5 for the year ending 30 June 19X6.

   Debit   £50   increase expenses (insurance)
   Debit   £50   increase assets (prepaid insurance)
   Credit £100   decrease assets (cash)

   ↑£50   ↑£50

   $$A + X \quad \equiv \quad L + E' + R$$

   ↓£100

3. Fred wishes to recognize (i.e. record) the charge for electricity for December 19X5. He has not yet received the bill but he estimates that the electricity charge for the month will be £30.

   Debit   £30   increase expenses (electricity expense)
   Credit £30   increase liabilities (electricity payable)

   ↑£30   ↑£30

   $$A + X \quad \equiv \quad L + E' + R$$

4. Fred pays wages of £200 for the week ending 1 July 19X5. The treatment of this transaction depends on whether Fred has already recognized the expense (and hence the liability) as in 3 above.

   (a) Assume that he has not recognized the expense.

   Debit   £200   increase expenses (wages expense)
   Credit £200   decrease assets (cash)

   ↑£200

   $$A + X \quad \equiv \quad L + E' + R \ldots (A)$$

   ↓£200

   (b) Assume that he has already recognized the expense, in which case the transaction would be as follows:

Debit   £200   decrease liabilities (wages payable)
Credit £200   decrease assets (cash)

$$A + X \quad \equiv \quad L + E' + R \ldots (B)$$

$\downarrow£200$ $\downarrow£200$

The original entry would have been of the same form as in 3 above, giving us:

$\uparrow£200$ $\uparrow£200$

$$A + X \quad \equiv \quad L + E' + R \ldots (C)$$

Combining (B) and (C) we get

$\uparrow£200$ $\uparrow£200$

$$A + X \quad \equiv \quad L + E' + R$$

$\downarrow£200$ $\downarrow£200$

i.e.

$\uparrow£200$

$$A + X \quad \equiv \quad L + E' + R$$

$\downarrow£200$

which is identity (A) above.

Should Expenses be Recognized before they are Paid?

When a business receives the benefit of services before paying for them the correct* treatment is to recognize the expense continuously. Thus the business should recognize expenses before they are paid. However, many businesses do not (with one important exception) use this approach. They use the short cut of only recognizing the expense when the payment is made, as illustrated in Example 3.2.4. The important exception is the need, when preparing an income statement, to ensure that all the expenses relating to the period are recorded whether they have been paid or not.

Debits and Credits — Summary

A debit is that aspect of a transaction which involves

an increase in assets, or
a decrease in liabilities, or
a decrease in owners' equity which may result from
       — the withdrawal of capital
       — an increase in expenses
       — a decrease in revenue.

* In the sense that such a procedure ensures that the accounting records would show, at each point in time, the required amounts of liabilities and owners' equity.

A credit is that aspect of a transaction which involves

> a decrease in assets, or
> an increase in liabilities, or
> an increase in owners' equity which may result from
>> — the introduction of captial
>> — a decrease in expenses
>> — an increase in revenue.

THE LEDGER AND T ACCOUNTS

The ability to differentiate between debit and credit is not, of itself, of any use. The important task is keeping track of individual assets, liabilities, revenue and expense headings and owners' equity.

To do this we can use ledger accounts where all entries relating to a particular type of asset, liability, etc., are brought together. This may be a page in a book, a card or a small part of a computer store. The ledger is the collection of ledger accounts, the book, the tray of cards or a larger part of the computer store.

We shall describe ledger accounts in greater detail later, but now it will be sufficient to introduce you to a slimmed-down version called the *T account*. The T account is a useful tool in the learning of double-entry book-keeping but experienced accountants often use T accounts to analyse or explain an accounting entry since they do convey sufficient information for many purposes.

The T account is so named because it looks like this:

Debit (Dr)	Credit (Cr)

To record a transaction we must first analyse it in debit and credit form and then record the debit part of the transaction on the left-hand side of the appropriate T account and the credit part on the right-hand side of its T account, as shown in Example 3.3.

Example 3.3

Record the purchase, for cash, of a motor car costing £1,000. The entry is:

    Debit Motor car   £1,000
    Credit Cash   £1,000
    and the T accounts will be:

                          Motor car
    _____
                         £
            Cash   1,000

	Cash
	£
	Motor car 1,000

In this example, each entry has been annotated by referring to the account which forms the other part of the double entry. This is not usually done in an actual book-keeping system, but it is the practice when using T accounts for teaching and for analysing transactions, and we shall adopt this useful device.

Note that if we want to find out the total in any account, i.e. the amount of the asset, liability, etc., we can do so by looking at the balance on the account. If the debits exceed the credits the account is said to have a debit balance and vice versa.

There are no rules in the United Kingdom concerning the detail necessary when deciding what ledger or T accounts to use. For example, should there be a ledger account for each motor vehicle or will one account recording all motor vehicles be sufficient? Should there be one or two ledger accounts for postage and stationery, etc? In general, the answers to such questions depend on the requirements of the particular business. There are many customary practices but at this stage the reader should rely on his intelligence and on the examples that will be provided.

We end this chapter with a longer example of the use of T accounts.

Example 3.4

1. The proprietor starts the business by paying into the firm's bank account the amount of £10,000:

Bank	*Capital*
£			£
Capital 10,000			Bank 10,000

2. The proprietor also pays £50 cash into the business to meet small items of expenditure:

Petty cash*	*Capital*
£			£
Capital 50		Bank 10,000	
		Petty	
		cash 50	

* Petty cash is used to describe actual cash on hand as opposed to the balance at the bank.

3. The firm purchases goods for resale for £2,000, on credit:

Inventory			*Creditors*	
£				£
Creditors 2,000				Inventory 2,000

4. The firm sells the above goods for £2,300, on credit:

Sales		*Debtors*	
	£	£	
	Debtors 2,300	Sales 2,300	

Inventory		*Cost of sales*	
£	£	£	
Creditors 2,000	Cost of sales 2,000	Inventory 2,000	

5. Having engaged staff, the firm pays £100 in wages, drawing the money from the bank:

Wages		*Bank*	
£		£	£
Bank 100		Capital 10,000	Wages 100

6. The firm pays out £5 for sundry small expenses:

Expenses		*Petty cash*	
£		£	£
Petty cash 5		Capital 50	Sundry exp. 5

7. Fixtures and fittings are purchased for £1,000, payment being by cheque:

Fixtures and fittings			Bank			
	£			£		£
Bank	1,000		Capital	10,000	Wages	100
					Fixtures and fittings	1,000

8. The proprietor withdraws £1,000 for his own use:

Drawings			Bank			
	£			£		£
Bank	1,000		Capital	10,000	Wages	100
					Fixtures and fittings	1,000
					Drawings	1,000

9. A creditor is paid £1,500 by cheque:

Creditors				Bank			
	£		£		£		£
Bank	1,500	Inventory	2,000	Capital	10,000	Wages	100
						Fixtures and fittings	1,000
						Drawings	1,000
						Creditors	1,500

10. A debtor pays £1,800 by cheque:

Debtors				Bank			
	£		£		£		£
Sales	2,300	Bank	1,800	Capital	10,000	Wages	100
				Debtors	1,800	Fixtures and fittings	1,000
						Drawings	1,000
						Creditors	1,500

EXERCISES

3.1 Analyse the following transactions in debit/credit form showing, in each case, that the extended accounting identity is maintained, e.g.

Williams acquired a motor car, for £1,000 cash, on 1 February 19X5.

Debit   £1,000 increase assets (motor car)
Credit   £1,000 reduce assets (cash)

↑£1,000

$$A \quad + \quad X \equiv L + E' + R$$

↓£1,000

Treat each of the following transactions separately.

In each case the accounting period is the six months ended 31 March 19X5.

1. On 3 November 19X4 Williams sold goods, for £700 cash, the cost of the goods to him being £500.

2. He received a legacy of £200 which he paid into his business bank account on 7 February 19X5.

3. He ordered a new van costing £900 on 15 March 19X5.

4. He received £1,300 from a customer on 1 November 19X4 in settlement of a debt.

5. In December 19X4 Williams sent the wrong type of widget to Smith. The widgets, which had cost Williams £250, were invoiced to Smith at £300. In January, Smith drew Williams's attention to the error and Williams agreed the fault was his. Smith, who had not paid for the widgets, returned the goods to Williams in January. Analyse the January transaction.

6. As (5) except that Smith had paid for the goods before discovering the error.

7. Williams paid, on 20 December 19X4, a subscription to a trade association of £1,000 for the year ended 31 December 19X5.

8. Williams paid his rent in arrears. On 2 January 19X5 he paid £500 for the quarter 1 October 19X4 to 31 December 19X4. Assume that he had not previously recognized the expense.

9. As (8) but assume that he had previously recognized the expense. Analyse the transaction involving the payment of the rent.

10. On 13 October 19X4 Williams withdrew £50 from his business bank account for his own use.

11. Some of the widgets sold on 5 November 19X4 by Williams to Jones were defective. The selling price of the widgets was £1,000, the cost price, £800. After some correspondence, Williams agreed, on 1 December, that the matter would be settled by his reducing the selling price from £1,000 to £950. Jones had not paid for the goods by 1 December. Analyse the December transaction.

12. Davies ordered 2 gross of super widgets from Williams in December 19X4. Since Williams did not know Davies, he asked Davies to pay a deposit of £300 which Davies did on 18 December 19X4; Williams thereupon ordered the goods from his supplier on 20 December 19X4. He received the goods on 5 January 19X5; the goods cost Williams £450. Williams sent the widgets to Davies on 12 January, invoicing him for £600. Williams paid his supplier on 10 February 19X5 and Davies paid Williams the balance due on 22 February 19X5. Analyse all the above transactions.

13. Williams had paid an insurance premium of £2,400 for the year ending 30 June 19X5 in June 19X4, i.e. the balance on the prepaid insurance account at 1 October 19X4 (being the asset as at that date) was £1,800. He wishes to recognize the insurance expense for the six months period ended 31 March 19X5.

3.2 There are a number of errors in the T accounts shown below. Note the transactions have been numbered in chronological order and that the cash account is correct.

Required:

(a) List the errors and show the corrected T accounts.
(b) Show that, after correcting the errors, debits = credits.

Capital

			£
		1. Cash	10,000

Cash

	£		£
1. Capital	10,000	2. Inventory	450
5a. Sales	800	7. Sundry expenses	20
8. Debtors	1,500	10. Motor vehicles	4,000
		12. Creditors	800

Cost of goods sold

	£		£
5b. Inventory	500	6b. Inventory	1,200

Creditors

	£		£
3. Motor vehicles	2,000	4. Inventory	1,000
12. Cash	800	11. Inventory	900

Debtors

	£		£
5a. Sales	800	9. Sales	300
6a. Sales	2,000		
8. Cash	1,500		

Inventory

	£		£
2. Cash	540	5b. Cost of goods sold	500
4. Creditors	1,000		
6b. Cost of goods sold	1,200		
11. Creditors	900		

Motor Vehicles

	£		£
10. Cash	4,000	3. Creditors	2,000

Sales

	£		£
9. Debtors	300	5a. Cash	800
		6a. Debtors	2,000

3.3 Using the information given in Exercise 2.5:
(a) record the transactions in T accounts;
(b) show that the total of the debits equals the total of the credits.

4 | Books of Prime Entry, the Trial Balance and the Preparation of Financial Statements

We should now see how the data actually flows through the accounting system. The system that we shall describe is a very basic one; of course in practice many variations and sophistications are introduced but the basic points will appear in all systems. This is true even for the ultimate — at the time of writing — a computerized system.

The first question to be answered is 'What events do we record?' The smart student may reply 'Easy, any changes affecting the firm's assets or liabilities'. But we do not record all the firm's assets and liabilities; for example, we record the firm's cash balance but not, with the present state of the art, the morale of the firm's employees. We do not even record all the changes affecting those assets and liabilities which we do recognize; for example, we do not, in conventional accounting, generally take any notice in the accounts of the increase in the market price of an asset.

So what do we record? It is not possible to give a short answer, because there is no concise theory of accounting. We can only refer you to the previous chapters, especially our discussion of accounting conventions in Chapter 1. However, we must point out that there are many events which are of considerable importance to the firm but which do not get recorded in the conventional double-entry accounting system.

BOOKS OF PRIME ENTRY

Data can first become recorded in all sorts of places; 'The Contribution of the Back of a Fag Packet to the Development of Accounting' is one of the great unwritten works of our time. However, that is not what we mean by a book of prime entry.

The Journal

Essentially a book of prime entry is the place where the transactions are summarized in debit and credit form with a view to being transcribed (or *posted* to use the jargon) into the ledger accounts. The essential features of a book of prime entry are illustrated in Figure 4.1. The functions of the columns shown there are described below.

Figure 4.1

(i)	(ii)	(iii)	(iv)	(v)
Date		*Fo.*	£	£
1 Apr X2	Motor vehicle account	M. 1	7,500	
	Costalot Limited	C. 1		7,500
	(Creditor)			

Being the purchase of a motor vehicle on credit per invoice number 75,326 and Director's Minute 357.

  (i) It is useful to know when.
 (ii) The names of the accounts to be debited and credited. It is the custom to put the account to be debited first and to indent the name of the account to be credited.
(iii) These are numbers of the ledger accounts; they make it easier to find the entry at a later date. Fo. is short for folio or page.
(iv) The amount to be debited.
 (v) The amount to be credited. It is necessary to repeat the figures because a transaction may, for example, require us to debit an account with £7,500 (as above) but to credit more than one account, e.g. Cash £500 (Deposit), Creditor £7,000. The total of the credits must be £7,500 of course.

We finish with a narrative which explains what we are doing and which should state the authority for us to do it.

A book of prime entry of this type is called a *journal* and can be used to give the necessary instructions to incorporate any sort of transaction in the ledger. We should repeat here that although the journal is in debit/credit form it is not an account — merely a set of instructions.

Other Daybooks

It would be extremely tedious to prepare journal entries of the above type for every one of the firm's transactions. So, special types of journal are used when a firm has a considerable number of transactions of the same type. For example a firm will probably purchase a large number of items on credit, so these will be recorded in a special journal called the *purchases daybook* (or purchases journal). An outline of such a book is shown in Figure 4.2.

Figure 4.2 Purchases Daybook

Date		Invoice Number*	Fo.	£
1 Jan X2	Whataprice Limited	37,432	W.4	1,253
1 Jan X2	Rising Prices & Co. Ltd.	37,433	R.2	642
.	.	.	.	.
.	.	.	.	.
.	.	.	.	.
31 Jan X2	Too Much Limited	37,611	T.5	6,231
				£153,432

* The purchaser stamps his own number on the supplier's invoice which accounts for the fact that the numbers are all in sequence.

The accounts of the suppliers are credited individually but the total of the credit purchases for January, £153,432, is posted to the debit of the inventory account in one figure. The time interval does not have to be a month of course.

Most firms will also have a sales daybook or sales journal to record the sales made on credit.

The Wages Book

One book of prime entry which most businesses find necessary is the wages book. A salaries book recording the salaries of monthly paid staff is often kept separately but it is used in exactly the same way as the wages book.

A wages book is shown in Figure 4.3. Its outstanding feature is its complexity, which arises from the Government's insistence that the business must act as an (unpaid) collector of taxes and contributions to the National Insurance scheme.

Gross pay is the amount which would be payable to the employee in the absence of deductions. It might include bonuses and overtime, etc., in addition to basic pay, and some companies show items other than basic pay in a separate column or columns. This is for the information of both the employee (whose pay slip is usually a duplicate of his entry in the wages book) and the employer.

The next set of columns details the deductions. PAYE stands for Pay As You Earn and is the employee's income tax which the employer must calculate and pay over to the Inland Revenue. National Insurance (NI) is the contribution which the employee must make to the scheme. The employer adds the above deductions to his own NI contribution (see below) and makes one payment to the Collector of Taxes.

An employee may agree that his employer can make other deductions from his wages for such things as trade union contributions, savings, etc. If this is the case, the wages book would have to be provided with additional deduction columns.

Net pay is gross pay less deductions and is the paltry amount which the employee actually receives.

The last column represents the contribution which the employer is forced to make to the National Insurance scheme.

When the wages book has been written and added up, the totals are posted as follows:

	Debit	Credit
Gross pay	Wages expense account	
Deductions – PAYE – National Insurance		Inland Revenue (creditor)
Net pay		Wages payable (creditor)
(Note: since gross pay = net pay plus deductions the debits will equal the credits)		
Employers' contributions National Insurance	Wages expense account	Inland Revenue (creditor)

The creditor accounts will be cleared as follows:

PAYE
National Insurance $\Big\}$ Monthly payment by cheque to Collector of Taxes

Wages payable   The payment of the net wages

Figure 4.3 The Wages Book

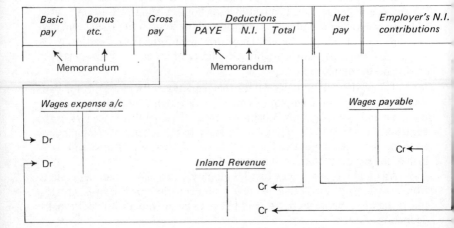

In each case the cash account will be credited and the creditor accounts debited. We are then left with one account, the wages expense account, which will show the wages expense for the period.

The Cash Book

This is also a book of prime entry but it can differ from the ones that we have looked at so far. For the cash book may also be an account forming part of the double-entry system. We should mention here that the cash book does not record cash but is concerned with the firm's bank account which may be an asset but which can be a liability, i.e. an overdraft. The book of prime entry/account which deals with actual cash is the *petty cash book*.

How can the cash book be both a book of prime entry and an account? Say, for example, a cash sale is made: the entry on the debit side of the cash book records the increase in an asset (or the reduction of a liability if the firm has an overdraft); but the entry is also an instruction to make a posting to a ledger account, in this case to the credit of the sales account. The same principle applies to the petty cash book. The treatment of cash discounts in the cash book is an exception to the above but we will not burden you with it at this stage.

Many firms use the cash book and petty cash books as straightforward books of prime entry in that they provide both debit and credit instruction. In such cases, ledger accounts will be maintained to record the balance at bank and cash in hand.

The relationship between the books of prime entry and the ledger accounts is illustrated in Figure 4.4.

Figure 4.4

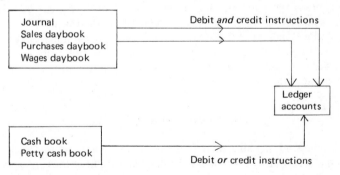

THE TREATMENT OF ROUTINE TRANSACTIONS

The entries in the daybooks will be made regularly and at intervals, say monthly, quarterly or annually, the totals will be cast where necessary and the postings will be made to the ledger accounts.

To cast is accountant's terminology meaning 'to add up'. (It is, you must remember, important for a profession to use phrases that no one else will understand.)

THE LEDGER

The basic function of a ledger account was described earlier when we presented the T account, but it will be useful to reintroduce the topic at this stage. One form of a ledger account, which may be described as the traditional form, is presented in Figure 4.5.

Figure 4.5

X Account

Date		Fo.	£	Date		Fo.	£
30 Jun X5	Journal	37	47·20	30 Sep X5	Cash book	117	35·93

You will notice that the basic structure of the T account has been maintained. You will (or should) remember that debit entries are made in the left-hand column. The dates may either be the actual date of the transactions or the date to which the postings are made (i.e. the date shown would be the end of the month or quarter, etc.).

The narrative columns show the book of prime entry which originated the entry and the folio (Fo.) columns tell us on which page of the book we shall find the entry. However, when learning accountancy or when using T accounts to help in the analysis of accounting problems, it is often useful to enter the name of the other account forming part of the double entry in the narrative column (see Chapter 3). This can be most helpful for many purposes, and we shall use this method. But the narrative column of a real live ledger account should give the source of the entry, since this makes it easier to trace it in order to understand its meaning and to find the evidence or authority supporting it.

THE TRIAL BALANCE

We have emphasized that all transactions have a dual aspect and that each transaction is recorded so as to ensure the debit and credit entries are equal in amount. So if the book-keeper has carried out his task correctly, in this respect at least, the total of the debit entries in the ledger should equal the total of the credit entries.

The main function of the trial balance is to see whether this is the case. It could be done by adding up all the debit entries in the ledger accounts (which may include the cash book and petty cash book) and comparing this total with the total of the credit entries. However, we can do it another way which we find much more useful; we compare the total of the debit balances with the total of the credit balances and if the totals are the same our task is completed and we say that the 'trial balance balances'.

We must be clear as to what is implied by the balancing of the trial balance. (We say 'implied' and not 'proved' because there are such things as compensating errors; they do happen and can have very embarrassing consequences.) The balancing of the trial balance implies the following:

1. The total of the debit entries equals the total of the credit entries, and
2. the arithmetic leading up to the computation of the balances on the accounts has been correctly carried out.

But there are of course a number of possible errors that would not be revealed by the check. These include:

1. The complete omission of a transaction.
2. Debiting or crediting the wrong account.

You should be able to think of others. Normally a trial balance would be prepared after the posting of all the routine transactions for a period.

THE PREPARATION OF FINANCIAL STATEMENTS

The trial balance also serves as a most useful starting point for the preparation of the financial statements (the income statement and balance sheet). We shall return to this in a later section after we have introduced some important topics, e.g. depreciation. However, it will be useful at this stage if we indicate the remaining steps that need to be carried out in order to prepare the statements. The stages may be summarized as follows:

Reversing Entries

The asset accounts which represent prepaid expenses at the start of the accounting period and the liability accounts which represent expenses payable at the start of the period must be examined. We shall consider these separately.

The Asset Accounts   Part or all of the prepaid expenses will have been used up during the accounting period and this transformation must be recorded, as illustrated in Example 4.1.

Example 4.1

Accounting period, year ended 31 December 19X5. The balance of £300 on the prepaid insurance account represents the premium for the period 1 January 19X5 to 31 March 19X5. Clearly the asset has been used up; so we transfer the opening balance to the expense account.

Journal entry		£	£
1 Jan X5	Insurance expense	300	
	Prepaid insurance		300
	Being the reversal of the opening balance		

T Accounts

Prepaid insurance

		£			£
1 Jan X5	Balance	300	1 Jan X5 Insurance		
			expense		300

Insurance expense

		£		£
1 Jan X5	Prepaid			
	insurance	300		

The Liability Accounts   In some cases it is convenient to leave the opening balance on the liability account and simply clear it by posting the cash payment to the liability account. However, in other cases it may be better to transfer the opening balance to the expense account; this is usually done when the payment is greater than the liability, i.e. when the payment both settles the liability and includes the payment of expenses of the current period. It is probably sensible to be consistent and use the reversal method in all cases, so reducing the chance of making mistakes. Example 4.2(b) shows this method.

Example 4.2

Accounting period, year ended 31 December 19X5. The balance on the wages payable account on 1 January 19X5 of £300 represents the wages owing for 29, 30 and 31 December 19X4. The first wages payment of 19X5 is £750 which covers the period 29 December 19X4 to 4 January 19X5. The alternatives are:

(a) No reversing entry

Journal*

		£	£
4 Jan X5	Wages payable	300	
	Wages expense	450	
	Cash		750
	Being payment of wages		

* As explained above cash payments are not usually dealt with through the journal but they are, for illustration, so dealt with in this example.

T account (other than cash)

Wages payable

		£			£
4 Jan X5	Cash	300	1 Jan X5	Balance	300

Wages expense

		£
4 Jan X5	Cash	450

(b) Using a reversing entry

Journal

		£	£
1 Jan X5	Wages payable	300	
	Wages expense		300
	Being the reversing entry		
4 Jan X5	Wages expense	750	
	Cash		750
	Being the payment of wages		

T account (other than cash)

Wages payable

		£			£
1 Jan X5	Wages expense	300	1 Jan X5	Balance	300

Wages expense

		£			£
4 Jan X5	Cash	750	1 Jan X5	Wages payable	300

You should note that the overall effect of each alternative is the same.

The Routine Transactions

The routine transactions, having been recorded in the day book, are posted to the ledger accounts.

End-of-period Adjustments

If any expenses for the period have not been recorded, the appropriate entry has to be made, i.e. by debiting the expense account and crediting the payable account. There are other end-of-period adjustments which will be described in a later chapter.

After all the above steps have been carried out, a trial balance can usefully be prepared. If we assume that the trial balance balances and that no errors of the sort that would not be disclosed by the balancing test have been made, we can easily produce the financial statements. We can select the revenue and expense items from the trial balance, thus obtaining the income statement for the period, while the balances on the asset, liability and permanent owners' equity accounts (the last after adjusting for the profit and loss for the period) give us the balance sheet. This is illustrated in Example 4.3.

Example 4.3

The following is the balance sheet of Lucky Jim at 1 January 19X5.

	£	£
Assets		
Inventory		1,000
Debtors (trade)		2,000
Rates prepaid		200
Cash		500
		£3,700
Financed by:		
Liabilities		
Creditors (trade)	800	
Wages payable	20	820
Owners' equity		
Lucky Jim Capital account		2,880
		£3,700

The following transactions took place in the month of January 19X5.

1. Goods costing £900 were purchased on credit.
2. Goods which cost £1,400 were sold on credit for £1,900.
3. Cash received from customers — £2,900.
4. Cash paid to suppliers — £1,000.
5. Sundry expenses for the month, all paid in cash, £80.
6. Lucky Jim's drawings for the month amounted to £100.
7. Wages paid during the month, £200.
8. Wages owing at the end of January, £15.
9. Rates expense for the month, £30.

All the above transactions will be analysed in journal form.

	Fo.	£	£
Wages payable	W2	20	
Wages expense	W1		20
Reversing entry			
Inventory	I1	900	
Creditors (trade)	C4		900
Note 1			
Debtors (trade)	D1	1,900	
Sales	S1		1,900
Cost of goods sold	C3	1,400	
Inventory	I1		1,400
Note 2			
Cash	C2	2,900	
Debtors (trade)	D1		2,900
Note 3			
Creditors (trade)	C4	1,000	
Cash	C2		1,000
Note 4			
Sundry Expenses	S2	80	
Cash	C2		80
Note 5			
Drawings	D2	100	
Cash	C2		100
Note 6			
Wages expense	W1	200	
Cash	C2		200
Note 7			
Wages expense	W1	15	
Wages payable	W2		15
Note 8			
Rates expense	R1	30	
Rates prepaid	R2		30
Note 9			

In the T accounts which follow, the opening balances are shown as well as the postings from the journal. The balances as at 31 January 19X5 are shown in **boldface figures** which are put on the debit or credit sides of the T account depending on whether the balance is a debit or credit balance.

C1   *Capital*

			£
		Opening balance	2,880
			2,880

C2   *Cash*

	£		£
Opening balance	500	Creditors (trade)	1,000
Debtors (trade)	2,900	Sundry expenses	80
		Drawings	100
		Wages expense	200
	3,400		1,380

2,020

C3   *Cost of goods sold*

	£		£
Inventory	1,400		

1,400

C4   *Creditors (trade)*

	£		£
Cash	1,000	Opening balance	800
		Inventory	900
	1,000		1,700

700

D1   *Debtors (trade)*

	£		£
Opening balance	2,000	Cash	2,900
Sales	1,900		
	3,900		2,900

1,000

D2   *Drawings*

	£	
Cash	100	

100

I1		*Inventory*		
	£			£
Opening balance	1,000	Cost of goods sold		1,400
Creditors (trade)	900			
	1,900			1,400

500

R1		*Rates expense*		
	£			£
Rates prepaid	30			

30

R2		*Rates prepaid*		
	£			£
Opening balance	200	Rates expense		30

170

S1		*Sales*		
	£			£
		Debtors (trade)		1,900

1,900

S2		*Sundry expenses*		
	£			£
Cash	80			

80

W1		*Wages expense*		
	£			£
Cash	200	Wages payable		20
Wages payable	15			
	215			20

195

W2		*Wages payable*	
	£		£
Wages expense	20	Opening balance	20
		Wages expense	15
	—		—
	20		35
			15

The trial balance as at 31 January 19X5 can now be prepared. Income statements are indicated thus — I.S., while balance sheet accounts are labelled B.S.

Trail Balance as at 13 January 19X5

		Debit £	Credit £	I.S. or B.S.
C1	Capital account		2,880	B.S.
C2	Cash	2,020		B.S.
C3	Cost of goods sold	1,400		I.S.
C4	Creditor (trade)		700	B.S.
D1	Debtors (trade)	1,000		B.S.
D2	Drawings	100		B.S.
I1	Inventory	500		B.S.
R1	Rates expense	30		I.S.
R2	Rates prepaid	170		B.S.
S1	Sales		1,900	I.S.
S2	Sundry expenses	80		I.S.
W1	Wages expense	195		I.S.
W2	Wages payable		15	B.S.
		£5,495	£5,495	

Having completed the above, it is a simple matter to prepare the income statement and balance sheet.

Lucky Jim

Income Statement

month ended 31 January 19X5

	£	£
Sales		1,900
less Cost of goods sold	1,400	
Wages expense	195	
Rates expense	30	
Sundry expenses	80	1,705
Net profit for the month		£195

Balance Sheet as at 31 January 19X5

		£	£
Assets			
	Inventory		500
	Debtors (trade)		1,000
	Rates prepaid		170
	Cash		2,020
			£3,690
Financed by:			
Liabilities			
	Creditors (trade)	700	
	Wages payable	15	715
Owners' equity			
	Capital account as at 1 January 19X5	2,880	
add	Profit for the month	195	
		3,075	
less	Drawings	100	2,975
			£3,690

Closing Entries

These accounts are interim accounts since, in our example, the income statement does not cover the whole year and so no closing entries would be made in the books. If, however, the income statement had covered the year, there would be one last step to make, transferring the balances on the temporary owners' equity accounts to the owners' capital account while the balances on the assets, liabilities and permanent owners' equity accounts are carried down.

So that we can illustrate the stage, we will show how it would be completed for our example while stressing that, in practice, it would normally be done only at the end of the firm's accounting year.

A journal entry should be used to initiate the transfer of the balances on the temporary owners' equity, and this entry is shown in Figure 4.6 together with examples of the appropriate ledger entries.

Note that the transfer to the capital account in Figure 4.6 has been described as 'income statement'. This is because an account called income statement (or, more often in the United Kingdom, profit and loss account) may be opened in the ledger and the balances on the temporary owners' equity accounts are transferred to that account. The balance on that account represents the profit (if it is a credit balance) or loss (debit balance) for the

Figure 4.6

	Fo.	£	£
Sales	S1	1,900	
Cost of goods sold	C3		1,400
Wages expense	W1		195
Rates expense	R1		30
Sundry expenses	S2		80
Capital account (being the profit for the period)	C1		195

S1			*Sales*	
		£		£
Income statement		1,900	Debtors (trade)	1,900

W1			*Wages expense*	
		£		£
Cash		200	Wages payable	20
Wages payable		15	Income statement	195
		£215		£215

period and this balance is then transferred to the capital account. Very often nowadays this account is omitted, but the description of the transfer being made to the income statement or profit and loss account is retained.

No journal entry is required to bring down the balances of the remaining accounts since balancing an account is not an entry in the books but simply a restatement of what is already there. Figure 4.7 illustrates the conventional way of bringing down the balance.

Figure 4.7

I1			*Inventory*		
		£			£
Opening balance		1,000	Cost of goods sold		1,400
Creditors (trade)		900	Balance	c/d	500
		£1,900			£1,900
Opening balance	b/d	500			

(c/d, carry down; b/d, brought down)

The only point that could lead to difficulty is that 'above the line', a debit balance is written on the credit side but this is merely a convenient way of showing that the balancing processing has been carried out — it shows the amount by which the credits would have to be increased in order to equal the debits, i.e. the debit balance.

EXERCISES

4.1 (a) Give three examples of book-keeping errors which will, in the absence of compensating errors, be disclosed by the non-balancing of a trial balance.

(b) What sort of book-keeping errors will not be disclosed by the trial balance test?

4.2 Bill started business on 1 January 19X4 and rented a shop from that date on the following terms:

1. Rental £300 per month, payable in arrears every four months, i.e. at the end of April, August and December.

2. Rates are payable in advance for six months on 1 April and 1 October.

When taking over the shop, Bill had to pay rates of £400 to cover the period 1 January 19X4 to 31 March 19X4. The rates charged for the years ended 31 March 19X5 and 19X6 were £1,000 and £1,200 respectively.

Bill's accounting year end is 30 June.

(a) Assume that all payments are made on the due dates.

Required:

Show for the period ended 30 June 19X4 and the year ended 30 June 19X5 the following ledger accounts:

> Rent expense,
> Rent payable,
> Rates expense, and
> Rates prepaid.

(b) Assume that Bill was short of cash and hence failed to pay the rent when due. The actual payments were:

> 8 August 19X4   £1,200
> 11 November 19X4 £1,000 and
> 18 March 19X5   £1,300

Required:

Using appropriate ledger accounts, record the rent transactions for the period to 30 June 19X4 and the year ended 30 June 19X5.

4.3 The following trial balance was extracted from the books of P. G. Forresthall as at 31 December 19X5:

	£	£
Balance at bank	800	
Capital account at 1 January 19X5		2,300
Cash in hand	120	
Cost of goods sold	8,000	
Insurance — expense	300	
— prepaid	50	
Inventory	900	
Sales		12,540
Sundry expenses	500	
Sundry expenses payable		100
Trade creditor — Smith		400
— Jones		200
Trade debtor — Jeeves	820	
— Drone	20	
Wages	3,930	
	£15,440	£15,540

Forresthall's book-keeper noted the difference in the trial balance and opened an account, which he called 'difference on trial balance account', debiting it with £100.

Forresthall noted this account, sacked the book-keeper, and called in a firm of accountants who made extensive tests in the course of which they discovered the following:

1. Forresthall had introduced capital of £100 in June 19X5; it had been credited to the sales account.

2. Wages payable of £70 as at 31 December 19X5 were completely omitted from the above.

3. The debit side of the cash book had been undercast by £200.

4. After a physical count of the inventory it was agreed that it should be restated at £880.

5. A cash sales of £60 had been debited to cash but had not been credited.

6. Of the £50 balance on the insurance prepaid account, £20 was the balance at the start of year representing the premium for the period 1 January 19X5 to 30 June 19X5.

7. Forresthall's drawings of £3,000 had been debited to wages expense.

8. A payment of £20 received from Jeeves had been posted to the debit of his account.

9. In December Forresthall paid Smith £90 for goods, but because the goods concerned had been mislaid, their purchase had not been recorded nor had they been included in the inventory check referred to in (4) above.

10. Some goods sold to Drone in November 19X5 for £50 had proved to be defective and Forresthall agreed that the price charged to Drone should be reduced by £30; this had not been reflected in the books.

Required:

(a) Prepare journal entries to record the above corrections.

(b) Prepare a corrected trial balance as at 31 December 19X5.

(c) Prepare Forresthall's income statement for the year ended 31 December 19X5 and his balance sheet as at that date.

4.4 The following balances appeared in the books of J. Wag at 1 January 19X6 after the preparation of the financial statements for 19X5:

	£	£
Balance at bank		300
Capital account		800
Electricity payable		15
Inventory	645	
PAYE and National Insurance payable		20
Rates prepaid	40	
Trade creditors – Black		300
– Brown		100
Trade debtors – Ford	600	
– Bridge	250	
	£1,535	£1,535

1. During the month ended 31 January 19X6:

  (a) Wag made the following purchases:

From Black	10 January £500	18 January £700
From Brown	12 January £300	17 January £200

  (b) He made the following sales:

Cash sales	11 January	£750
Credit sales		
Ford	20 January	£600
Bridge	12 January	£900
Raft	15 January	£1,100

2. A physical check of the inventory at 31 January revealed an inventory of £450 stated at cost.

3. Wag employs only one worker, T. Last. Last's wage slips for the four pay days in January were as follows:

Date	Gross wages	Income tax	National Insurance	Net wages
	£	£	£	£
Friday 5 January	30	3	2	25
Friday 12 January	36	4	2	30
Friday 19 January	30	3	2	25
Friday 26 January	30	1	2	27

The net wages were paid on the above dates.

4. Assume that the employer's contribution to the National Insurance scheme is £3 per week.

5. The additional wages payment for the week ending 12 January was for overtime. Last did not do any more overtime in January.

6. Cash receipts for the month:

		£
11 January	Cash sales	750
12 January	Ford	550
21 January	Bridge	1,000

7. Cash payments for the month (in addition to net wages):

		£
2 January	Black	300
5 January	Brown	100
15 January	Collector of taxes	20
18 January	Electricity (based on the meter reading on 10 January)	30
26 January	Drawings	400
31 January	Sundry expenses	100

8. Rates expense for January, £8.

9. Electricity used in the period 11 − 31 January was £13.

Required:

(a) Record the above in the following books of prime entry:

   Purchase daybook
   Sales daybook
   Wages book

    Cash book
    Journal

(When designing the wages book, assume that it is to be used by a firm employing some 20 workers.)

(b) Post from the books of prime entry to the ledger accounts.

(c) Prepare Wag's trial balance at 31 January 19X6.

(d) Prepare Wag's income statement for the month ended 31 January 19X6 and his balance sheet as at that date.

5 | Matching: The Accrual Concept

The life of a firm is continuous from the date it starts business to the date that it is finally wound up. It would be relatively easy to prepare a set of accounts for the whole life of the business. We would measure the resources that the owner put into the firm and compare the total with the resources that he has withdrawn, including those released from the ultimate disposal of the business. We could then compare his increase in 'well-offness' (i.e. his profit) with that which he could have achieved had he engaged in a different activity. However, Fred will not be overjoyed if, after 50 years of sweat and toil, he is told he should have put his money into a building society. We obviously need to provide the owners of a business, and others, with information while there is still time to do something about it, i.e. during the life of the business. If you are still not convinced of the need, remember that the end of a business is not always voluntary; it might, for example, run out of cash. Now the provision of regular accounting reports will not prevent a business running out of cash, but it will make it more difficult for even an obtuse management to slide down the road to bankruptcy.

The need to produce accounting reports during the life of a business is clear; we must, therefore, divide our long continuous time into digestible and usefully sized chunks. However, the task of breaking down the ongoing stream into small (time) sections gives rise to most of the problems (but much of the interest) in financial accounting.

Our first task is to break up the time stream into sections. Ideally the periods selected should be such that the results of one time period can be reasonably compared with the results of other time periods.

All firms produce annual accounts — a good choice so far as comparability is concerned, since the effect of seasonal variations is eliminated. Tax regulations make the preparation of annual accounts necessary, and entities whose affairs are more closely controlled by law than a sole trader, e.g.

limited companies, must, under the provisions of the Companies Acts, produce annual accounts.

But if 'a week is a long time in politics' then a year can be eternity for a business; so accounting reports need to be prepared more frequently for management purposes: quarterly, monthly or even weekly.

We have now decided to divide our operations into periods for information purposes; so we must decide which figures to include in any given period. Suppose that our task is to report, in the form of accounts, on the results of year 5 in the life of a firm. We must produce the accounts in a meaningful way; this implies that they must be internally consistent and comparable with year 4 and indeed any other year.

It is straightforward common sense (often the best guide in accounting but too seldom used) that if we include in the accounts of year 5 the revenue applicable to that year we must, to make sense of the accounts, include the expenses relating to that revenue and therefore to that year.

It follows that if we have used the same criteria in preparing year 4 accounts (and in due course year 6 accounts) the results of year 5 will be comparable with the results of year 4 (and in due course year 6).

How shall we achieve this desirable end? First we need to examine closely the meanings of *revenue* and *expense*.

REVENUE

Revenue is the gross (i.e. before the deduction of expenses) increase in assets that takes place as the result of selling goods or providing services. By applying the basic accounting equation, we can observe that this increase in assets results in a corresponding increase in owners' equity.

If a shop sells a packet of pins for 3 pence for cash there is an increase in assets (cash of 3 pence) and this is the revenue. There is of course a decrease in assets, the pins, but we shall deal with this under expenses. If this important transaction were conducted on credit, the creation of the debtor for 3 pence is the revenue; in this case the later payment of 3 pence would not constitute revenue but would simply be a change in the composition of a firm's assets.

EXPENSE

A useful starting point is the observation that a business is a vehicle for the transformation of assets. A business acquires assets which are, in general, used up in the revenue-earning process. There are two important factors, the acquisition of an asset and its use. The asset will have an historical cost*, i.e. the amount that is paid or will be paid in order to acquire

---

* There are other sorts of cost but when cost is used without an adjective the writer usually means historical cost.

it, but until it is used the ownership of an asset does not give rise to an expense. An expense for a period may be defined as the amount of the asset that has been used up in the revenue-earning process. An asset at a point in time, say at the end of an accounting period, is then the amount that has not yet been used up; an asset is often referred to as being the *unexpired cost,* the expense being the *expired cost.* Occasionally assets are used up other than in the revenue-earning process, e.g. some fool loses them or some knave pinches them; such unpleasant expirations of costs are known as losses. Mathematically we have:

Historical cost of asset	−	Expense (or loss) for the period	=	Asset at the end of the period

and for the next period:

Asset at the start of the period	−	Expense (or loss) for the period	=	Asset at the end of the period

and so on until the asset is finally consumed.

This highlights the link between the balance sheet and income statement. That part of the cost of an asset which is not treated as an expense (or loss) will appear as an asset in the balance sheet.

As an example, suppose that a trader purchases for resale goods amounting to £5,000 in year 4; he sells no goods in year 4 but he does sell half of them in year 5; in year 6 goods with an historical cost of £200 are eaten by the office cat (acts of God and cats are not covered by this trader's insurance policy) but the rest of goods are safely sold. So we have for year 4:

Historical cost of asset	−	Expense (or loss) for the period	=	Asset at the end of the period
£5,000	−	0	=	£5,000

for year 5:

Asset at the start of the period	−	Expense (or loss) for the period	=	Asset at the end of the period
£5,000	−	£2,500	=	£2,500

and for year 6:

£2,500	−	£2,500*	=	0

Note that the above does not depend on when the business actually paid for the goods.

ACCRUAL ACCOUNTING

To return to the problem with which we started this chapter: we must divide the firm's activities into different time periods. This means that we

* Expense £2,300, loss £200.

must decide in what time period the revenue from a particular transaction should be placed and determine the total of the expenses for each time period. The normal practice is not to use the receipt and payment of cash as the criteria for the recognition of revenue and expense. Instead a method known as *accrual accounting* is used. Accrual accounting is based on two key conventions: the realization and matching conventions.

The Realization Convention

'Revenue should not be Recognized until it is Realized' — the key here is: when is it realized? Think of all the steps that a trader must go through in selling an item. He must:

1. Decide to deal in a particular line of goods.
2. Find a source of supply.
3. Buy the goods either for stock or against a specific order which means that he would have first to find a customer.
4. Have the goods transported to him.
5. If the order was for stock, bring the goods to the attention of potential customers.
6. Sell the goods.
7. Collect the cash.

And if that seems long-winded, imagine what a similar list for a manufacturing company would look like.

Before he started, the trader certainly had no profit from the deal; at the end, hopefully, he has. When did the profit arrive: gradually throughout the transaction or at a particular point of time? The realization convention holds that the profit comes all in a rush at point 6; the moment the goods are sold (i.e. when the ownership of the goods is transferred) is considered to be the time at which the revenue is realized. Up to and after this stage each step will simply result in changes within and between the assets and liabilities; only at point 6 is there a net increase in owners' equity. So putting figures to our example we might have:

3. Buy the goods for £100

Increase assets, inventory	£100
Increase liabilities, creditors	£100
(or decrease assets, cash £100)	

4. Transport of the goods for £10

Increase assets, inventory	£10
Increase liabilities or decrease assets	£10

6. Sell the goods on credit for £150

Increase assets, debtors	£150 → *Revenue*
Decrease assets, inventory	£110
Increase owners' equity	£40

Following 6 we are back to changes in assets

7. Increase assets, cash   £150
    Decrease assets, debtors   £150

Although the other steps in the process might well involve expenditures, we have assumed that they are either immaterial or of such a nature that it is not possible to identify them with a particular transaction.

Is this rule that the profit is earned when the goods are sold (or service rendered) a reasonable one? Let us look at some of the arguments that have been advanced in its favour.

1. *The transaction is completed.* Not really, since the cash has not been collected.

2. *Selling is the most difficult part of the whole operation.* It may be so in some circumstances but not always. Recently a car dealer had no difficulty in selling a well-known type of car; the difficulty was first to get one. There are many other such examples; so difficulty in selling does not have sufficient generality to support the rule.

3. *For the first time in the operation the enhanced value of the asset can be objectively determined.* We are getting warmer. What value should we place on our inventory before it is sold? It might be reasonable to take a figure in excess of historical cost, thus recognizing some profit. But how much more than historical cost and correspondingly how much profit? The trader might have his own estimate, but that would be personal or subjective. It is only when the goods are sold that someone else enters the picture and provides an independent valuation, i.e. the customer who has agreed to pay £150 for the goods. This valuation is considered sufficiently objective to be recorded in the accounting system; the importance of objectivity has been stressed elsewhere in this book. Of course the valuation is not completely objective as there is some risk that the debt will not be paid. The value of the debt depends on the probability that it will be paid. This must be sub-jectively estimated, e.g. observer X might say that there is a 99 per cent chance that the debt will be paid, valuing it at £148·50, while observer Y, believing that there is a 98 per cent chance of payment being made, would value the debt at £147. But then no measure is completely objective; the point is that the measurement we have used is, in most circumstances, considered to be objective enough.

Objectivity then is probably the best justification of the realization convention although the results of using it are not completely acceptable.

It is artificial to recognize the profit from a transaction at one moment of time, when the profit is the result of a whole transaction involving many steps and possibly a long duration. A detailed exposition of this point is beyond the scope of this book but is bound up with the whole problem of valuation. However, we should add that the rule that profit is taken when the goods are sold or service rendered is quite often broken. To give two of the more important examples:

1. Companies engaged on large contracts, e.g. civil engineering companies, may in some years complete only a few jobs while in other years they may complete a large number. If they followed the general rule, the profit figures would be like a yo-yo and, as this is considered undesirable, such companies often depart from the rule and recognize some of the profit before the end of the job.
2. It is a sad fact that hire purchase and similar companies do not always manage to collect the cash, and so such companies often relate the recognition of profits to the collection of cash rather than to the sale.

The Matching Convention

This convention tells us that we should recognize the expenses incurred in earning revenue in the same time period as we recognize the revenue.

We have already described an expense as the amount of the asset that has been used up in the revenue-earning process. The matching convention and this definition say very much the same thing.

Expenses can be divided into *product expenses* (or product costs as they are usually called) and *period expenses* (or period costs). Product costs are those which can be specifically identified with a particular bundle of goods or a particular service. In the case of a retailer, the product costs would be the goods themselves and, possibly, the cost of bringing the goods to the point of sale, the costs of maintaining the goods in sound condition and the costs of selling them. (These latter costs always exist, but often it is not possible to identify them with particular goods, in which case they are treated as period costs.) A manufacturing company would have many more product costs.

Period costs, conversely, are all those expenses which cannot be readily associated with particular units. So the transformation from asset to expense is done on the basis of time rather than on the basis of particular dollops of revenue.

A simple example might help. Suppose a trader carries out the following transactions:

January   1 No opening inventory
           2 Buys goods (A) for £20
          10 Buys goods (B) for £10
          30 Sells goods (A) for £35
              Rent for the month £11

February   1 Buys goods (C) for £30
          10 Sells goods (B) for £16
              Rent for the month £11

Then we would have for the months of January and February:

	January £ £	February £ £	Convention
Revenue	35	16	*Realization*
less Product cost	20	10 ⎫	
Period costs	11 31	11 21 ⎬	*Matching*
Net income for the month	£4		
Net loss for the month		£5	

These are essentially the income statements for the months of January and February, but they do not follow the usual form.

   One essential point to remember is that it does not matter whether cash has entered into all, some or none of the above transactions. The income statements would be the same in any case; of course the balance sheet would differ. This point is so important that we will take the risk of beating it to pulp, in Example 5.1.

Example 5.1

Consider a stall-holder in one of those new market halls. Other than the rent paid to the local council (his only period cost) all transactions are for cash. Each month revenue less product costs comes to exactly £100 (that is what he tells the Inland Revenue; we don't believe it either). The rent is £240 per year payable in advance for the year on 1 January. Assume that the trader starts business on 1 January with a capital of £50 all in cash. His balance sheet at 1 January is:

Capital	£50	Cash	£50

We will trace his history by looking at a series of balance sheets, the income statement for each month being the same:

	£
Revenue less product costs	100
less Rent	20
Net income for the month	£80

   The trader received his rent demand on 1 January, his first day of trading, but he did not get round to paying it in January. So his balance sheet at the end of January could be presented as follows:

	£		£
Capital	50	Cash	150
Retained earnings	80		
Creditor for rent	20		
	£150		£150

However, this is not the complete picture, since he has a contractual obligation to pay £240. The expense is still only £20 but if we recognize the liability of £240 we must also recognize an asset of £220 being the prepaid rent (a bad phrase in the circumstances) which represents that part of the £240 which has not been used up. Taking this into consideration we get the following balance sheet at the end of January:

	£		£
Capital	50	Cash	150
Retained earnings	80	Prepaid rent	220
Creditor for rent	240		
	£370		£370

The Council is not best known for speed and the rent was not paid in February; so the balance sheet at the end of February was:

	£		£
Capital	50	Cash	250
Retained earnings	160	Prepaid rent	200
Creditor for rent	240		
	£450		£450

He did not pay the rent in March but by this time he had received one or two mild reminders. In April the letters became more frenzied, so he paid; the balance sheet at the end of April was:

	£		£
Capital	50	Cash	210*
Retained earnings	320	Prepaid rent	160
	£370		£370

	£
* Capital	50
4 months cash @ £100 per month	400
	450
less Rent	240
	£210

As time passes, the asset — prepaid rent — reduces by £20 per month as it is transferred into an expense.

This section headed 'accrual accounting' has introduced the twin conventions — realization and matching — which constitute the method. It should be compared with the cash basis, where revenue is recognized when the cash is received and expenses are recognized when the cash is paid.

EXERCISES

5.1 What have assets and expenses in common? How do they differ?

5.2 Black started business on 1 January 19X1 as a bridge builder. In the period 1 January 19X1 to 31 December 19X8 he completed the following contracts:

Year in which the contract was completed	Contract number	Value of contract, i.e. revenue
		£000
19X2	1	80
19X3	2	84
19X3	3	120
19X5	6	10
19X7	4	160
19X7	5	150
19X7	7	70
19X8	8	150

He had no work in progress as at 31 December 19X8.

The following table shows the expenditure for each year analysed among the different contracts. It also shows 'general overheads', i.e. expenditure which Black could not conveniently allocate to the various contracts:

Year	Total	1	2	3	4	5	6	7	8	General overheads
					(£000)					
19X1	50	20	10							20
19X2	100	20	10	40						30
19X3	127		40	40	10					37
19X4	69				20	25				24
19X5	66				10	25	8			23
19X6	133				40	25		30		38
19X7	121				20	25		10	30	36
19X8	88								60	28
	754	40	60	80	100	100	8	40	90	236

A consulting civil engineer visited a number of the sites on 31 December of some years and issued certificates showing his estimates of the 'value' of the work done to date. The following schedule gives details of the certificates issued:

Date	Contract	(£000)
31 Dec X2	2	30
31 Dec X2	3	60
31 Dec X4	4	35
31 Dec X5	4	50*
31 Dec X5	5	40
31 Dec X6	4	100*
31 Dec X6	5	70*
31 Dec X6	7	40
31 Dec X7	8	35

*These are cumulative figures

(a) Show Black's profits for the years 19X1 to 19X8 inclusive using the following methods:

> (1) The revenue for each contract is recognized in the year in which the contract is completed (i.e. all the profit on a contract is taken in the year in which the contract is completed).

> (2) Black estimates the total profit on each contract and allocates that profit between the years on the following basis:

> Profit recognized during the year

> $$= \text{Estimated total profit} \times \frac{\text{Expenditure on contract for the year}}{\text{Estimated total expenditure}}$$

> Assume that Black's estimates are completely accurate

> (3) Uncompleted contracts are 'valued' on the basis of the certificates or, if one has not been issued, on the total expenditure to date.

(b) Discuss the comparative advantages and disadvantages of the above methods.

5.3 Towards the end of 19X3 Sid purchased a plot of land, known as Lake Rise, on which he proposed to build, for sale, a number of houses. His architects drew up the following plan:

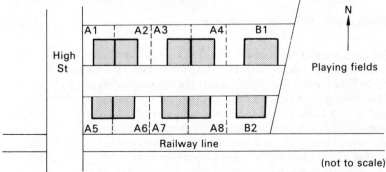

The following estimates were made of the revenue and costs for this development:

Revenue		£	£	£
Detached houses	B1	38,000		
	B2	34,000		
			72,000	
Semi-detached houses				
A1		24,000		
A2,A3,A4 – 3 @ £26,000		78,000		
A5		20,000		
A6,A7,A8 – 3 @ £22,000		66,000	188,000	
			260,000	

Costs			
Purchase of land (including legal expenses)		60,000	
Levelling of land		10,000	
Roads and services		30,000	
Construction costs			
Semi-detached houses 8 @ £6,000	48,000		
Detached houses 2 @ £11,000	22,000	70,000	
Selling expenses			
General promotional expenses		4,000	
Commission to estate agents (10% of selling price)		26,000	30,000	200,000
Estimated profit on the development				£60,000

Sid has a number of other developments on hand and he employs a small number of 'head office' staff including the architects. Sid's architects were fairly hard pressed with work on existing projects and so when the Lake Rise development appeared, Sid was persuaded to engage an additional architect at a salary of £5,000 per annum. Sid's chief architect's argument was that although the Lake Rise development would not, in itself, use up the whole time of the new man, his employment would mean that the quality of the work on the other projects could be improved. In addition, the new man would be very useful when work started on a major new development which was expected to start in 19X5. Accordingly, a new architect was engaged on 1 January, 19X4.

The levelling costs referred to above were mainly caused by the need to remove a small hillock on the site of house B1.

Work started on the Lake Rise development in January 19X4 and by the end of 19X4 the following payments had been made:

	£	£
Purchase of land		60,000
Levelling of land (completed)		12,000
Roads and services (uncompleted)		20,000
Construction costs		
B1 (completed)		12,000
B2 (uncompleted)		4,000
A3 (completed)		7,000
A4 (completed)		6,000
A8 (uncompleted)		2,000
General promotional expenses		3,000
Agents' commission B1	3,800	
A4	2,600	6,400
Damage caused to a neighbour's property due to a mishap with a bulldozer (not covered by insurance)		5,000

During 19X4 Sid sold B1 and A4 for the original estimated prices. By the end of 19X4 Sid was running short of cash and so in order to sell quickly the other completed house, A3, he offered to pay the purchaser's legal expenses. He sold A3 on these terms at the end of 19X4 and the purchaser's legal expenses are estimated to amount to £1,000.

Discuss the problems involved in estimating Sid's profit or loss for 19X4 on the Lake Rise development. In your answer you should attempt to provide at least one estimate of Sid's profit or loss.

5.4 St. John is a professional man who has hitherto produced his accounts on a cash basis (i.e. revenue is recognized when the cash is actually received and expenses are recognized when they are paid).

His income statement (on a cash basis)* for the year ended 30 June 19X5 is as follows:

---

*Income statements based on cash accounting are usually called receipts and payments accounts.

	£	£
Fees		18,000
less Rent	1,200	
Rates	800	
Secretary's wages (including National Insurance)	2,800	
Sundry expenses	2,000	6,800
Surplus		£11,200

During the year St. John withdrew £10,000 from his business bank account to pay his living expenses.

St. John was persuaded by his accountant to change from cash to accrual accounting and it was decided that the new basis should be applied for the year ended 30 June 19X5. The following information as at 1 July 19X4 is relevant:

	£
Debtors for fees	6,000
Business bank account (overdrawn)	4,000
PAYE and NI payable	20
Rent payable	200
Prepaid rates	300

Fee income (on an accrual basis) for the year ended 30 June 19X5, £21,000. Rent expense (on an accrual basis) for the year ended 30 June 19X5, £1,200. As at 30 June 19X5:

	£
PAYE and NI payable	12
Prepaid rates	400

(a) Prepare (on the basis of the information provided) St. John's balance sheet as at 30 June 19X5 and his income statement for the year ended on that date.

(b) Are there any other assets or liabilities which you might expect to find?

(c) What arguments might St. John's accountant use when persuading him to change from cash to accrual accounting? Are there any counter arguments?

6 | *Matching: Depreciation and Bad Debts*

In this chapter we shall deal with two important applications of the matching convention; the treatment of long-lived assets (depreciation) and of bad and doubtful debts.

FIXED AND CURRENT ASSETS

Before dealing with depreciation it is necessary to discuss the distinction between fixed and current assets.

Current assets are cash and those assets which the firm's management intends and can reasonably expect to convert into cash, sell or consume within a year (or within the normal trading cycle of the firm if longer than a year). Current assets normally consist of the following:

inventory (which will be sold)
debtors (which will be converted into cash)
prepaid expenses (which will be consumed)
cash itself.

The main point about *fixed assets* is that they are not intended to be used up within the year. A second feature is that they are held to further the main trading activities of the firm. This distinguishes fixed assets from certain assets such as investments in other companies which are not directly related to the trading activities of the firm and which the management does not intend to realize within the year. Such assets are considered to be neither fixed not current, but there is no generally agreed name for them.

Fixed assets consist of such assets as land, buildings, plant and machinery, fixtures and fittings. However, we must emphasize that the classification of an asset depends on the way in which it is to be used rather than on the nature of the asset; so, for example, a motor car may be a fixed asset (e.g. a salesman's car) or a current asset (part of the stock of a motor dealer).

We should now introduce the terms revenue and capital expenditure. *Capital expenditure* (an unfortunate phrase seeing how often we come across the word capital) is that used in acquiring or improving fixed assets, while *revenue expenditure* is that which will be converted into an expense or become a current asset.

We hope that we have not made the distinction between fixed and current assets, and the corresponding distinction between capital and revenue expenditure, too clear, because there are many practical and theoretical difficulties in distinguishing between them. For example, how should we treat expenditure on an existing asset? The general principle is that if the purpose of the expenditure is to maintain the asset in its original condition the expenditure is treated as revenue expenditure, but if its purpose is to improve the asset we have a capital expenditure and the result is an increase in fixed assets. However, a major overhaul of a vehicle or machine, in addition to returning the asset to its original condition, will often result in an element of improvement as well, and apportioning the total expenditure into its two components can prove difficult. In practice it is often found that no attempt at apportionment is made, the whole of the outlay being regarded as revenue expenditure.

METHODS OF DEPRECIATION

By definition, fixed assets are those assets which will provide services over a number of years and the matching convention tells us that we should recognize the asset in the same periods as we recognize the associated revenue. Thus we must not write off, or expense, the whole cost of the asset in the period in which the asset is acquired, but should instead convert the asset into an expense over its life. This gradual conversion is known as *depreciation*.

How should we compute the depreciation charge for each year? An obvious way would be to compare the current value of an asset at the end of the year with its value at the start of the year and say that the difference is depreciation. But as we have already emphasized, traditional accounting practice is based on historic cost and not current values; consequently that method is generally not acceptable. The traditional approach is to estimate the total expenditure to be written off, i.e. the cost of the asset less its estimated scrap value, and then to write off that expenditure over the estimated life of the asset by using one of the methods that we shall describe below. The life of the asset is usually measured in time, but in some instances may be measured on the basis of actual usage.

In order to consider the difficulties inherent in estimating the life of an asset we should think about the reasons why most fixed assets, other than land, have a limited life. These reasons may be classified as physical wear and tear, and obsolescence. Obsolescence may be of the asset itself, e.g. a new machine may make the use of the original asset, an older machine, uneconomic because the new machine is faster or requires less labour. Obsolescence may also be caused by the object produced by the asset, if, for example, it goes out of fashion. In the latter case, the degree of obsolescence will depend on the specific nature of the asset; some assets may be easily adapted to alternative uses while others may have only one use, the original.

None of the above variables can be determined with any accuracy; obsolescence, in particular, is rapidly increasing in importance in our highly market-orientated and technological society.

Deciding how much should be written off and over what period is not the only problem, for there are a number of depreciation methods from which to choose. A firm's management must decide which one to employ, and a user of financial statements who wishes to compare the financial performance of a number of companies must appreciate the effects of the various methods.

In practice we find two main methods of depreciation – the *straight-line basis* and *accelerated depreciation*. There is another method, the annuity method, which takes account of the interest costs involved in investing in a long-lived asset; this method has many theoretical attractions but is rarely used.

Straight-line Basis

The total expected cost is simply spread over the number of years of expected service giving the amount of depreciation expense per annum:

$$\frac{\text{Original cost} - \text{Expected salvage value}}{\text{Expected number of years use}}$$

A variation on this method is the production unit basis which may be used when the life of the asset can be conveniently expressed in terms of the output. For example:

	£
Cost of machine	6,000
less Estimated scrap value	1,000
Cost to be written off	£5,000
Expected life	10,000 hours

If the machine is used for 4,000 hours in 19X5 the depreciation charge for that year is:

$$£5,000 \times \frac{4,000}{10,000} = £2,000$$

Accelerated Methods

With these methods the depreciation charge in the earlier years of use is greater than in the later years; the rationale for this approach is discussed on page 74. Accelerated methods include (a) Sum of the Years' Digits Method and (b) The Diminishing Balance Method.

Sum of the Years' Digits Method   Let n be the asset's life; the years are each represented by a digit: 1, 2, 3, 4, . . . n. Having fixed on n, the digits are summed and the fractions of the asset cost are charged to the years in reverse order so that the earlier years are charged more than the later years. For example, if the expected life is three years:

Year	*Digit*
1	1
2	2
3	3
Sum of digits	6
Total net cost	£12,000

The depreciation charges for each year are:

Year			£
1	3/6 of £12,000	=	6,000
2	2/6 of £12,000	=	4,000
3	1/6 of £12,000	=	2,000
			£12,000

The Diminishing Balance Method   Here the depreciation charge for each year is a fixed percentage of the 'book value' of the asset (cost less accumulated depreciation to date) at the start of the year. For example:

Cost of the asset £10,000

Fixed percentage 20%

	£
Cost of asset	10,000
Depreciation charge year 1 20% of £10,000	2,000
Book value at the start of year 2	8,000
Depreciation charge year 2 20% of £8,000	1,600
Book value at the start of year 3	6,400

and so on.

The fixed percentage which will write down the asset approximately to its estimated scrap value over the required number of years can be found from the following formula:

$$r = \left(1 - \sqrt[n]{\frac{s}{c}}\right) 100$$

where r is the desired rate, n the number of periods of expected asset life, s the expected salvage value and c the cost of acquisition.

Comparison of Methods

Example 6.1

Cost of asset £5,250. Estimated salvage value £250. Estimated life 5 years.

Periods	Straight-line		Sum of years' digits		Diminishing balance*	
	Opening balance	Charge for period	Opening balance	Charge for period	Opening balance	Charge for period
	£	£	£	£	£	£
Year 1	5,250	1,000	5,250	1,667	5,250	2,395
Year 2	4,250	1,000	3,583	1,333	2,855	1,302
Year 3	3,250	1,000	2,250	1,000	1,553	708
Year 4	2,250	1,000	1,250	667	845	385
Year 5	1,250	1,000	583	333	460	210
Balance	250		250		250	
Total depreciation		£5,000		£5,000		£5,000

* The fixed percentage is 45·62 per cent.

There are two possible justifications for the use of accelerated methods:

1. It may be assumed that the revenue which the asset helps to generate falls as the asset gets older and that, following the matching convention, it is reasonable to charge higher depreciation in the years in which the revenue is higher and vice versa. Although it is true that in some cases revenue will fall, e.g. if competitors bring out a rival product, it should be noted that this fall will, in general, be irregular and there is little reason to suppose that the fall will follow the same path as the reduction in the depreciation charge.
2. As the asset gets older, the maintenance costs increase; so the use of accelerated depreciation means that the total expense in each year will be approximately constant. Obviously it would be a considerable coincidence if this happened.

Straight-line depreciation may be justified when the contribution made by the asset remains roughly constant over its life; however it is likely that the main reason why straight-line depreciation is the most widely used method in the United Kingdom is that it is simple and easy to understand.

In the United States accelerated depreciation is much more popular because its use gives a considerable taxation advantage: a greater charge against taxable income is allowed in the earlier years of ownership; so the payment of tax is delayed. In the United Kingdom this does not happen because for taxation purposes depreciation is replaced by capital allowances, the rates of which are specified by the taxation statutes and are not affected by the depreciation method used by the tax-paying company.

A Practical Note   In practice, assets are, in general, not written off over a period which reflects their exact expected life. Instead they may be classified into, say, 'five-year assets' (to be written off over five years), 'ten-year assets' etc., and an asset is allocated to the class which best approximates to its expected life. Very large assets may, however, be dealt with on an individual basis.

THE RECORDING OF DEPRECIATION

We shall now examine the methods used to record depreciation, by using the following information:

Cost of asset	£10,000
Purchased on	1 January 19X2
Estimated life	3 years
Estimated scrap value	£1,000
Depreciation method	Straight-line
Depreciation charge	£3,000 per annum
End of accounting year	31 December

When the asset is purchased it will be debited to the asset account. Since the purpose of depreciation is to convert the asset into expenses over three years at the rate of £3,000 per year it may be thought that the obvious way is to transfer £3,000 per year from the asset account to an expense account (and hence reduce owners' equity). Thus:

Asset account

		£			£
1 Jan X2	Cash	10,000	31 Dec X2	Depreciation expense	3,000
			31 Dec X2	Balance c/d	7,000
		£10,000			£10,000
1 Jan X3	Balance b/d	7,000	31 Dec X3	Depreciation expense	3,000
			31 Dec X3	Balance c/d	4,000
		£7,000			£7,000
1 Jan X4	Balance b/d	4,000	31 Dec X4	Depreciation expense	3,000
			31 Dec X4	Cash	1,000
		£4,000			£4,000

However, the above method is not as sensible as it seems, for we are hiding some useful information; for example, consider the information given by the account at 31 December X3, £4,000. It tells us that the cost less the accumulated depreciation to date is £4,000, but it does not tell us the cost or the accumulated depreciation. It would not be difficult to calculate that information in this simple example but, in general, it would be time-consuming to work out these facts each year.

A better method is to have two accounts, one showing the cost of the asset and one showing the accumulated depreciation. We would then have:

Asset, at cost, account

		£			£
1 Jan X2	Cash	10,000	31 Dec X2	Balance c/d	10,000
		£10,000			£10,000
1 Jan X3	Balance b/d	10,000	31 Dec X3	Balance c/d	10,000
		£10,000			£10,000
1 Jan X4	Balance c/d	10,000	31 Dec X4	Accumulated depreciation	9,000
			31 Dec X4	Cash	1,000
		£10,000			£10,000

Asset, accumulated depreciation, account

		£			£
31 Dec X2	Balance c/d	3,000	31 Dec X2	Depreciation expense	3,000
		£3,000			£3,000
31 Dec X3	Balance c/d	6,000	1 Jan X3	Balance b/d	3,000
			31 Dec X3	Depreciation expense	3,000
		£6,000			£6,000
31 Dec X4	Asset, at cost, account	9,000	1 Jan X4	Balance b/d	6,000
			31 Dec X4	Depreciation expense	3,000
		£9,000			£9,000

The overall effect of the two methods is the same; the depreciation charge is £3,000 per year and the net amount at which the asset is included in the records at the end of each year is the same. In the first method the amount is the balance on the asset account; with the second method the amount is found by deducting the balance on the accumulated depreciation account from the balance on the cost account. The difference between the balances is called the *net book value* (NBV); the use of the word value is a more than trifle unfortunate since this amount will in general not be the economic or current value of the asset.

The accumulated depreciation is called a *contra asset* account ('contra' meaning 'opposite' or 'to the contrary') and its purpose is to show how much of the asset has been converted into expense. Because of this relationship the balances on the account are displayed next to each other on the balance sheet, for example in the balance sheet at 31 December 19X3:

	£
Asset, at cost	10,000
less Accumulated depreciation	6,000
Net book value	£4,000

SALE OF A FIXED ASSET

When the asset has been disposed of, the cost and its accumulated depreciation have to be eliminated. In the method shown, the accumulated depreciation account is closed by transferring its balance to the cost account. This produces a debit balance on that account of £1,000; since this is exactly offset by the proceeds of the sale, the crediting of the cost account with £1,000 will close that account. This is an acceptable short cut only when the proceeds of sale exactly equal the net book value. However when, as will usually happen, the two are not equal, the short cut should not be used. The longer method is shown below.

If the sales proceeds are greater than the net book value, too much depreciation has been charged; if they are less, insufficient depreciation has been recognized. In the first case the sale of the asset will result in an increase in owners' equity and will be shown as a credit in the income statement, while in the second case the reverse will hold.

The best way of dealing with the sale of fixed assets is to open an account called the disposal of fixed assets account, or the like. The method is then:

1. Debit that account with the cost of the asset (the credit being to the asset, at cost, account).

2. Credit the account with the total depreciation charged on that asset to date (the debit being to the asset, accumulated depreciation, account).

The balance at this stage on the disposal of fixed assets account is the net book value (cost less accumulated depreciation) of the asset sold.

3. Credit the proceeds of sale to the disposal account (the debit being to cash, debtors, etc.).

The balance on the disposal account is now the difference between the net book value and the sales proceeds. If the difference is a credit, too much depreciation has been charged and if a debit, too little depreciation has been written off.

4. When the books are closed, the balance on the disposal account is written off to owners' equity via the profit and loss account.

This item is often described on the income statement as the profit (or loss) on the disposal of fixed assets. This is a stunningly bad description, since there is generally no question of there being a profit on the sale of the asset; there is either an excess depreciation charge written back or an additional depreciation charge, and it would be better if these items were described as such.

Suppose that the asset is sold for £8,000 on 1 March 19X3. Then we would have:

Asset, at cost, account

		£			£
1 Jan X2	Cash	10,000	31 Dec X2	Balance c/d	10,000
		£10,000			£10,000
1 Jan X3	Balance b/d	10,000	1 Mar X3	Disposal of fixed assets account	10,000
		£10,000			£10,000

Asset, accumulated depreciation, account

		£			£
31 Dec X2	Balance c/d	3,000	31 Dec X2	Depreciation expense	3,000
		£3,000			£3,000
1 Mar X3	Disposal of fixed asset	3,000	1 Jan X3	Balance b/d	3,000
		£3,000			£3,000

Disposal of fixed assets account

	£			£
1 Mar X3 Asset, at cost, account	10,000	1 Mar X3 Asset, accumulated depreciation, account		3,000
31 Dec X3 Owners' equity	1,000	1 Mar X3 Cash		8,000
	£11,000			£11,000

Additional Practical Points

Usually a separate pair of accounts is not opened for each individual asset; instead accounts are opened for different classes of assets. Typical classifications include freehold land and buildings; leasehold buildings; plant and machinery; fixtures and fittings; motor vehicles, etc. This degree of aggregation means that there are no details of individual assets in the double-entry system; these details can, and we hope always are, recorded in plant registers, etc.

In our example we have assumed that the firm recognized depreciation on an annual basis; however, some firms recognize depreciation at more frequent intervals, say monthly or quarterly. The principles are the same.

If an asset is purchased part way through the year the depreciation charge for the first year should, to follow the logic of the argument, depend on the time for which the asset is used. However, some firms, especially smaller ones, charge a full year's depreciation in the first year, no matter when the asset was acquired.

WHAT DEPRECIATION IS NOT

We should emphasize that depreciation is exactly what we said it was: the conversion of an asset into expenses over the periods in which the asset is used. Unfortunately the depreciation process is often given, by people who should know better, certain magical qualities, i.e. that it is a valuation exercise, and that it will help the firm to replace the asset when the time comes.

The first myth has already been dealt with, so we will confine ourselves to the second. The belief that depreciation is concerned with helping to ensure that the firm has sufficient funds available to replace assets is widely held, especially be managers and other practical men.

The first point to consider is that depreciation does not produce funds (or cash). Cash is obtained by selling goods and can not, unfortunately, be produced by the manipulation of book-keeping entries, no matter how complex they may be. It seems an obvious point, but we find that there are many who cannot accept it; so we will provide an example for any doubting Thomases.

Suppose a trader, all of whose transactions are on a cash basis, starts business on 1 January 19X1 with an initial capital, in the form of cash, of £100. Suppose further that he immediately purchases a fixed asset costing £100 which has a five-year life and a zero scrap value. The asset is to be depreciated on a straight-line basis, i.e. the depreciation charge is to be £20 per year. Assume that the business is a stable but unprofitable one and that the trader's income statement for each of the first five years is as follows:

		£	£
Sales			200
less Cash expenses		185	
Depreciation		20	
			205
Net loss			£5

At the end of five fruitless years he would have the following balance sheet:

	£		£
Capital	100	Fixed asset at cost	100
		less Accumulated	
		depreciation	100
			—
less Accumulated losses	25		
	—	Cash	75
	£75		£75

The 'proper' depreciation charge has been made, but there are insufficient funds available to replace the asset even if it is assumed that the replacement cost has not increased. But the depreciation charges are not even responsible for the retention of the paltry £75; that would have been there anyway, for if our trader had never heard of depreciation his balance sheet at the end of five years would be:

	£		£
Capital	100	Fixed asset, at cost	100
Retained earnings	75	Cash	75
	£175		£175

To reiterate: the only reason that cash of £75 is available is because the cash from sales exceeded the cash used to pay for operating expenses by £15 per year.

Some would argue that this is too naïve, because the relationship between depreciation and asset replacement is more subtle than may be implied from our discussion. Their argument is as follows:

1. One of the major purposes of computing net income is to help the owner decide how much cash he can withdraw from the business for consumption. We accept this.
2. Depreciation charges reduce the net income of the business and hence reduce the amount of cash that would be withdrawn. Depreciation therefore ensures that the business will have sufficient cash to replace the asset.

In reply we argue:

1. The net income figure is only one factor of many that should be considered when deciding how much cash to withdraw. A trader may take out more or less cash than is represented by retained earnings*. The other factors include his plans for the business and the amount of cash available in the business (one result of using accrual accounting is that the net income for a period will not, in general, result in an increase in cash of an equal amount).
2. The amount of cash that is left in the business is therefore the result of the consumption decision and not of the depreciation charge.
3. The cash left in the business may be used to finance an increase in stock and debtors, reduce the creditors or to acquire other fixed assets. In order to ensure that cash is available to replace the depreciating asset, it should be specifically earmarked and either put to one side (i.e. kept in a bank) or invested in liquid

* In the case of limited companies, amounts that can be paid to the owners – dividends – must not exceed the retained earnings.

assets. Again this is not part of the depreciation process, and to the extent that it is done (hardly ever), it results from the business's overall plans and forecasts.

In fact a business obtains the cash necessary to replace fixed assets in the same way as it obtains the cash required to purchase additional fixed assets — from one, or a combination, of the following:

Cash produced by operations
Borrowing
The introduction of additional capital

BAD AND DOUBTFUL DEBTS

It is sadly the case that there are some people and firms who cannot or will not pay their debts. A firm can minimize the distress caused by the non-payment of debts by taking great care before extending credit to its customers, but some companies are somewhat lax in their credit arrangements (some go so far as to give credit to students). Even in the best regulated firms, bad debts do occur and we shall now consider the various ways of accounting for them.

The simplest way would be for the firm to wait until that final awful realization that a customer will not return from his six-year holiday in Australia and pay the £50 he owes and, at that time, convert £50 of assets into an expense by making the following entries:

Debit   Bad debts expense £50 (i.e. recognize the expense)
Credit   Debtors £50 (i.e. reduce the asset)

However, this treatment does not comply with the matching convention, since the firm did not recognize the bad debts expense in the period in which it recognized the associated revenue; and of course with a bad debt the firm has not only failed to earn the expected profit but has also lost the cost of the goods sold.

To get over this problem, an estimate may be made, at the end of an accounting period, of the proportion of the outstanding debtors that will fail to pay. This estimate may be done on the basis of an individual examination of the specific debts or on the basis of a percentage of the outstanding debtors; the percentage may be found from experience or, quite often, by tradition (we always take 5 per cent).

Having obtained an estimate, a *provision for doubtful debts account* is set up, which acts as a contra-asset account (like the accumulated depreciation) to the debtors account.

Suppose that we have a new firm, or at least one that does not have an existing provision for doubtful debts account, and that our estimate for doubtful debts at 31 December 19X4 is 5 per cent of the debtors of £24,000. The journal entry to record this would be:

	£	£
Bad debts expense	1,200	
Provision for doubtful debts		1,200

We have recognized an expense and have, correspondingly, reduced an asset. However, since we have not given up all hope of receiving our money or, if the percentage method was used, have not identified the specific doubtful debts* the asset itself is not written down and so a contra asset account is used.

If in the next period bad debts amounting to £800 are actually written off, there need be no additional charge for bad debts, since it has already been made when setting up the provision account. The entry recording the writing off of the debt would be:

	£	£
Provision for doubtful debts	800	
Debtors		800

At the end of that accounting period the required balance on the provision for doubtful debts accounts is estimated. But now the expense will depend on the difference between the required and existing balance on the provision account. If the existing balance is greater than the required balance then there will be a credit to the income statement (increase in owners' equity) as the excess provision against doubtful debts is written back.

Example 6.2

Frank starts a business on 1 January 19X3.

Debtors:	31 December 19X3	£10,000
	31 December 19X4	£12,000†
	31 December 19X5	£ 4,000†

†After writing off the bad debts

Bad debts written off:

In 19X4 £700
In 19X5 £250

The required provision is 5 per cent of the outstanding debtors.

* Although this may be done for credit control purposes.

		Bad debts expense for year		Balance on provision account at the year end
		£	£	£
19X3	5 per cent of £10,000	£500		500
19X4	Opening balance on provision account		500	
	Bad debt written off (£700)	200	500	
	Required provision 5 per cent of £12,000	600		600
		£800		
19X5	Opening balance on provision account		600	
	Bad debts written off		250	
			350	
	Required provision 5 per cent of £4,000 = £200			
	So the credit to the income statement is:	£150	(150)*	200

*In accounting minus quantities are often indicated by putting the figures in brackets.

If we put the above in book-keeping terms the ledger account would be as follows:

Bad debts expense

		£			£
31 Dec X3	Provision for doubtful debts account	500	31 Dec X3	Owners' equity	500
		£500			£500
19X4	Debtors	200	31 Dec X4	Owners' equity	800
31 Dec X4	Provision for doubtful debts account	600			
		£800			£800
31 Dec X5	Owners' equity	150	31 Dec X5	Provision for doubtful debts account	150
		£150			£150

Provision for doubtful debts

		£			£
31 Dec X3	Balance c/d	500	31 Dec X3	Bad debts expense account	500
		£500			£500
19X4	Debtors	500	1 Jan X4	Balance b/d	500
31 Dec X4	Balance c/d	600	31 Dec X4	Bad debts expense account	600
		£1,100			£1,100
19X5	Debtors	250	1 Jan X5	Balance b/d	600
31 Dec X5	Bad debts expense account	150			
31 Dec X5	Balance c/d	200			
		£600			£600
			1 Dec X6	Balance b/d	200

EXERCISES

6.1 So far as the following fixed assets are concerned:
(a) What depreciation method do you think would be most appropriate and why?
(b) Discuss the ways in which obsolescence may affect the asset.

1. A delivery van used by a baker.

2. A filing cabinet.

3. A shop held on a 20-year lease.

4. A plastic moulding machine which has been specially constructed to manufacture a new novelty — plastic stetsons. It is expected that these will be all the rage next Christmas and thereafter sales will continue for a year or two but at a very much lower level.

5. Machine X. This machine is used by its owners as a standby machine when the normal machines are down for maintenance or have broken down. Occasionally machine X is used to increase capacity when there is a glut of orders. Machine X is of the Dumbo type, rarely used nowadays because modern machines are far more efficient. When these machines are operated at full capacity they last for about four years before they become completely worn out.

6.2 At 31 December 19X2 John's debtors owed him £10,000. He had not, up to this time, maintained a provision against doubtful debts account but now thought he should set one up and decided that he should base his provision on 5 per cent of the debtors. He made the necessary adjustment on 31 December 19X2.

The following figures relate to the years ended 31 December 19X3 and 19X4.

	19X3	19X4
	£	£
Sales	120,000	130,000
Cash received from customers	115,000	136,000
Bad debts written off	1,000	300
Cash received in respect of a bad debt written off in 19X3		200

(a) Prepare John's bad debts expense account and provision against doubtful debts account for the years ended 31 December 19X3 and 19X4.

(b) How would you treat the receipt of £200?

6.3 V. Rough purchased his first van, BYX 958 H, on 1 January 19X0 for £1,200. He purchased another van, CYX 713 J on 1 July 19X1 for £1,600.

On 1 May 19X2 Rough traded in BYX 958 H in part exchange for a new van. The relevant invoice is given below:

I Smooth Ltd

	£
Purchase of van NBG 111 K	1,773
Delivery charge	10
Number plate	5
Road fund licence	25
5 gallons of petrol	3
Sign-writing	12
	1,828
less Allowed in part exchange for van BYX 958 H	528
	£1,300

1. Rough depreciates his vans on a straight-line basis over four years and assumes that they will have a zero scrap value.

2. His year end is 31 December.

3. Taxes payable on the purchase of vans may be ignored.

Show for the period 1 January 19X0 to 31 December 19X2 Rough's

> Motor vans account
> Motor vans, accumulated depreciation, account
> Depreciation expense account
> Sale of fixed assets account

6.4 Mal's trial balance as at 30 June 19X2 was as follows:

	£		£
Debtors	1,610	Mal's capital account	
Cost of goods sold	9,800	as at 1 July 19X1	1,950
Drawings	2,140	Bank overdraft	450
Inventory	2,400	Creditors	1,400
Motor vehicle – at cost	1,800	Sales	16,200
Wages expenses	1,000	Provision against	
Sundry expenses	200	doubtful debts	100
Rent expense	1,100	Motor vehicle –	
Rates expense	240	accumulated	
Rates prepaid	360	depreciation as at	
		1 July 19X1	300
		Rent payable	200
		Wages payable	50
	£20,650		£20,650

1. The necessary reversing entries were not made at 1 July 19X1, e.g. the balance on the rent payable account represents the rent payable at 1 July 19X1.

2. The rent expense and rates expense for the year ended 30 June 19X2 were £1,200 and £480 respectively.

3. The depreciation charge for the year should be based on 20% of the reducing balance.

4. A physical check of the inventory at 30 June 19X2 revealed that it was £2,300 and not £2,400 as shown in the inventory account.

5. Bad debts of £30 should be written off and the provision against doubtful debts should be adjusted to 10% of the debtors.

6. Wages payable at 30 June 19X2 were £25.

(a) Prepare journal entries recording the above adjustments.
(b) Prepare a revised trial balance.
(c) Prepare Mal's income statement for the year ended 30 June 19X2 and his balance sheet as at that date.

6.5 Sally owns a small printing firm which has one large machine. You have been her accountant for some years when, one day, she rushes into your office waving a piece of paper and shouting. 'You fool. You've been making me depreciate my printing machine for years but now that it has worn out I find that I can't afford to replace it. Look'.

You inspect the piece of paper she proffers you and find that it is a corner which, in her rage, she has torn off her latest balance sheet. The fragment reads:

Fixed assets	Cost	Accumulated depreciation	NBV
	£	£	£
Printing machine	10,000	9,000	1,000
Van	1,000	800	200
	£11,000	£9,800	£1,200
Current assets			

You calm her down but she goes on. 'Look! All my estimates proved to be correct. The machine lasted for as long as I expected and I shall be able to trade it in for £1,000 as I told you when I bought it. Furthermore I have been very lucky in that the price of that particular type of machine has not gone up for years. What is going to happen when my van packs up? I'm told that the price of that sort of van has doubled since I got mine'.

Answer her.

7 | *Matching: Cost of Goods Sold*

It may be thought that the most straightforward application of the matching convention is to ensure that, when goods are sold, their cost is determined and that the goods sold are recorded by debiting the cost of sales account (recognizing the expense) and crediting the inventory account (reducing the asset).

But consider the following:

Slim started business on 1 January 19X4 and made the following purchases of goods for resale.

2 January	10 units @ £5 each	Purchase A
3 January	12 units @ £6 each	Purchase B
10 January	8 units @ £7 each	Purchase C*

Suppose that on 12 January Slim sells 5 units. What is the cost of that sale? A logical way of approaching the question is to ask which of the units were actually sold.

Suppose that the bundle sold consisted of 3 units from Purchase A and 2 units from Purchase C, then the cost of sales would be:

$$3 \times £5 + 2 \times £7 = £29$$

This method which is known as *actual cost* is practicable where a firm deals with only a relatively small number of units, but it will often be impossible to identify the source of the goods sold. It will therefore be useful to consider two special cases.

If it is assumed that goods are sold in the order in which they were acquired, i.e. the 'oldest' units are sold first, then the cost of goods sold would be taken to be:

$$5 \times £5 = £25.$$

* At one time we would have felt it necessary to apologize for using such an extreme example of rising prices to illustrate our argument, but nowadays perhaps no such apology is needed.

This method is known as *first in first out* (FIFO).

We might instead assume that the goods sold are those which have been most recently acquired (i.e. the 'youngest' items). The cost of sales would then be:

5 x £7 = £35.

This method is known as *last in first out* (LIFO).

An alternative approach would be to ignore the actual (or assumed) flow of goods and use the average cost of the goods in hand.

Total cost of 30 units   = £178·00
Average cost per unit   = £   5·93
Cost of sales 5 x £5·93 = £ 29·65

This method is known as *average cost*.

These three methods of matching the cost of sales to revenue will be discussed in greater detail below. However, we should say at this stage that the choice of the matching method may not depend on the physical flow of goods in the business. For example, first in first out may be used in circumstances when the goods sold are in fact those which were the most recently acquired.

PERPETUAL AND PERIODIC INVENTORY SYSTEMS

A perpetual system depends on the accounting system being sophisticated enough to be able to record the cost of sales as each item is sold. So, when a sale is made the necessary transfer between the cost of goods sold and the inventory account can be made. Thus at any time the balance on the inventory account will represent the actual inventory.

Although the use of a perpetual system has many advantages, it can be expensive to operate and so many firms (especially smaller businesses) use a periodic system. Here no attempt is made to determine the cost of goods sold each time a sale is made. Instead, at intervals which may be annual, the inventory is counted and the cost of goods sold for the period estimated. An omnibus entry debiting cost of goods sold and crediting inventory with the cost of goods sold for the period can be made on the following lines.

Balance on inventory account at 30 June 19X4
(representing the Inventory at 1 July 19X3   £
plus cost of purchases for the year to 30 June 19X4)   80,000

A physical check of the Inventory at
30 June 19X4 reveals an Inventory of   25,000

Cost of goods sold in year to 30 June 19X4   £55,000

The amounts at which the inventories at 1 July 19X3 and 30 June 19X4 are stated depends on the method used to determine the cost of goods sold.

We describe the above process as one which *estimates* the cost of goods sold, because of course some of them may not have been sold. They may have been stolen, deteriorated due to storage (e.g. evaporated) or lost.

Periodic systems do not allow the accountant to exercise the same degree of control as perpetual systems. Another great advantage of perpetual systems is that financial statements can be drawn up without the need to count the inventory.

Firms using a perpetual system will carry out physical checks of the inventory from time to time to see whether the balance on the inventory account accords with the actual situation. However, if separate records are kept for different types of inventory it will not be necessary to check the whole of the inventory at the end of the accounting period.

Although there is no reason why the periodic system could not be used with the method of accounting for inventories we have described so far, in practice this is rarely, if ever, done. Businesses using the periodic system use the alternative method for accounting for inventories, the 'stock/purchases' approach which we introduce in Chapter 10.

DETERMINING THE COST OF GOODS SOLD

We will now present extended examples of FIFO, LIFO and average. The same data will be used in each example.

No opening inventory

	Purchases	£		*Sales*
January	10 units @ £3·00	30		
April	20 units @ £3·50	70		
			May	6 units
October	12 units @ £4·00	48		
			November	22 units
	42 units	£148		28 units

Closing inventory = 42 − 28 = 14 units.

First In First Out (FIFO)

It is assumed that:

	£
All the goods purchased in January have been sold, 10 @ £3·00	30
as well as 18 units from the April purchase, 18 @ £3·50	63
So the cost of goods sold would be	£93

The closing inventory is assumed to consist of:

	£
2 units from the April purchase, 2 @ £3·50	7
and the whole of the October purchase, 12 @ £4·00	48
giving a closing inventory of	£55

It is often easier to work out the cost of goods sold by simply deducting the closing inventory from purchases, i.e.

	£
Purchases	148
less Inventory	55
Cost of goods sold	£93

In the more general case, where there is an opening inventory, purchases would be replaced by opening inventory plus purchases.

Last In First Out (LIFO)

In this method it is assumed that the closing inventory consists of the earliest purchases, i.e. all the January purchase and 4 units from the April purchase. So the closing inventory is:

	£
10 @ £3·00	30
4 @ £3·50	14
	£44

The cost of goods sold can be found as follows:

	£
Purchases	148
less Closing inventory	44
Cost of goods sold	£104

Average Cost

Average cost can be applied both on a perpetual and a periodic basis.

In the case of the periodic method, only one average cost is worked out for the period, and all the units are assumed to have been purchased at that cost. Thus:

Purchases	£148
Number of units purchased	42
Average cost per unit	£3·52
So the cost of goods sold = 28 x £3·52 =	£99
and the closing inventory = 14 x £3·52 =	£48

With the alternative, the perpetual method, a new average cost is computed after each purchase, and the cost of goods sold and inventory are priced on the basis of the latest average cost.

Note that the sale of units does not necessitate the recomputation of average cost. Thus:

Cost of goods sold
£

Average cost after January purchase

£3

Average cost after April purchase

10 @ £3·00	£30
20 @ £3·50	£70
30	£100

Average cost $\dfrac{£100}{30} = £3·33$

May sales 6 x £3·33	19·98

There are now 24 units left at an average cost of £3·33.

19·98

19·98

Average cost after October purchase

24 @ £3·33	£79·92
12 @ £4·00	£48·00
36	£127·92

Average cost $\dfrac{£127·92}{36} = £3·55$

November sales 22 x £3·55		78·10
		£98·08
Closing inventory 14 @ £3·55		£49·70

All the above methods are based on historical costs but they yield different figures. If you consider that the differences are too small to be material, imagine what they would look like if three noughts were added to the end of each figure.

The above example is a good illustration of the problems that beset traditional accounting practice. Even though objective historical cost is used, the profit disclosed will depend on the method of inventory 'valuation' used.

Further, if the above four inventory methods are coupled with the three depreciation methods outlined in Chapter 6 (and there are others) we can see that 3 x 4 = 12 different accounting profits could be derived from the same circumstances. Moreover the total of twelve can be increased a thousandfold if we consider other areas where judgement is required, e.g. the treatment of doubtful debts, research and development expenditure, long-lived contracts etc.

FEATURES OF THE ALTERNATIVE METHODS

We shall now return to the various methods, outline their features and discuss their acceptability.

Actual Cost

This method is strongly favoured where it is possible to identify the actual cost of the goods sold, because it is strictly in line with the physical flow of the goods. It is most suitable for firms which deal with goods that have a high unit value, such as motor vehicles, jewellery, etc. However, there is a potential danger where the inventory consists of identical units which, nonetheless, have been purchased at different prices. Then the management of the firm can easily manipulate the reported profit. For if they want to show a large profit they can decide that they have sold the cheapest units, while if they want to show a lower profit they can say that they have sold the most expensive items.

Actual (or unit) cost is used in the United Kingdom and is accepted by the Inland Revenue.

Average Cost

Average cost closely reflects the physical flow of goods in some cases, especially when inventories are in a liquid form. However, average cost is used in other circumstances. Its particular attraction is that it smooths out the effect of price changes.

Assume that the price of a particular type of goods has been constant for some time and then suddenly increases. With LIFO this increased price will be immediately reflected in the cost of sales. With FIFO the cost of sales would be based on the old, lower, price until all the old inventory is deemed to be sold. But then the cost of sales would immediately jump to the new level. With average cost, however, the cost of sales will be increased immediately, as a result of the recalculation of the average cost, but only a proportion of the increase will be reflected. This proportion will increase as the ratio of goods purchased at the new price to goods purchased at the original price increases. Thus it can be argued that average cost is particularly suitable for dealing with commodities where prices fluctuate rapidly.

Average cost is used in the United Kingdom and is accepted for taxation purposes.

First In First Out

The main advantage claimed for FIFO is that it is often a close approximation to the physical flow of goods. This is particularly true of a trader in perishable goods who goes to a good deal of trouble to ensure that the oldest items in his inventory are sold first.

Although a balance sheet is not intended to be a statement of value it should be pointed out that FIFO, being based on the most recent prices paid, will usually produce a balance sheet *inventory* figure which is a closer approximation to the current cost of its replacement than by any other method.

FIFO is widely used in the United Kingdom and is acceptable for tax purposes.

Last In First Out

The most important feature of LIFO is that, under certain conditions (constant or increasing physical volume of inventory) the LIFO *cost of goods sold* will be based on the most recent prices paid by the business and will in general provide in the income statement the closest possible approximation to the replacement cost of the goods sold, as at the date of sale,

without departing from the historical cost system. If the prices of the goods
concerned are rising, the LIFO cost of goods sold will be greater than, say,
the FIFO cost of goods sold, and hence the LIFO profit will be less than the
FIFO profit.

Example 7.1

Hank started business in 19X1 and made the following sales and purchases.

Year		Purchases	£	Sales
19X1	January	40 units @ £2	80	80 units
	June	60 units @ £3	180	
			£260	
19X2		100 units @ £4	£400	100 units
19X3		200 units @ £5	£1,000	160 units
19X4		100 units @ £6	£600	50 units

Inventory and cost of goods using LIFO and FIFO are shown below.

Year	Cost of goods sold		Year-end inventory	
	LIFO	FIFO	LIFO	FIFO
	£	£	£	£
19X1	220	200	40	60
19X2	400	380	40	80
19X3	800	780	240	300
19X4	300	250	540	650

One fairly convenient way of working out the above figures is:

LIFO

Year	Inventory at the year-end	Cost of goods sold = Opening inventory plus purchases less closing inventory
19X1	20 @ £2 = £40	£ 0 + £ 260 − £ 40 = £220
19X2	20 @ £2 = £40	£ 40 + £ 400 − £ 40 = £400
19X3	20 @ £2 = £40 40 @ £5 = £200 —— £240	£ 40 + £1,000 − £240 = £800
19X4	20 @ £2 = £40 40 @ £5 = £200 50 @ £6 = £300 —— £540	£240 + £ 600 − £540 = £300

FIFO

Year	Inventory at the year-end	Cost of goods sold = Opening inventory plus purchases less closing inventory
19X1	20 @ £3 = £60	£ 0 + £ 260 − £ 60 = £200
19X2	20 @ £4 = £80	£ 60 + £ 400 − £ 80 = £380
19X3	60 @ £5 = £300	£ 80 + £1,000 − £300 = £780
19X4	10 @ £5 = £ 50 100 @ £6 = £600	£300 + £ 600 − £650 = £250
	£650	

Note how, in Example 7.1, the LIFO inventory is built up in layers, there being a layer for each year in which more units are purchased than sold, for example:

Inventory at the end of 19X4

	£
19X1 layer 20 @ £2	40
19X3 layer 40 @ £5	200
19X4 layer 50 @ £6	300
	£540

Example 7.1 also illustrates that, under the assummed conditions, the LIFO inventory is less than the FIFO inventory because the LIFO inventory is based on older (and lower) prices; the fact that the LIFO inventory is based on old prices is one of the disadvantages of LIFO.

Having spent some time on LIFO we must now admit that it is rarely, if ever, used in the United Kingdom. It is widely used, however, in the United States and a number of Western European countries.

It is, perhaps, too cynical to observe that the attractions of LIFO have been more readily accepted in countries where there are tax advantages to be gained from its use, such as the United States, than in countries where no such advantage can be obtained, such as the United Kingdom. A tax advantage is obtained when the LIFO profit is less than the FIFO profit, i.e. increasing prices and constant or increasing physical volumes of inventory. These conditions existed in the United States over the last 30 or so years and it has been during that period that many American firms have adopted LIFO. The advantage is, of course, that as the recognition of profit is deferred the payment of tax is also deferred.

The fact that LIFO is not accepted by the British Inland Revenue does not in itself mean that British firms cannot use it. For they could prepare their financial statements on the LIFO basis and then adjust the profit for taxation purposes, with use of a method acceptable to the Inland Revenue. However, few British firms use LIFO, as the method does not meet with the approval of most British accountants. The reason for this is the British view that the cost of sales should, as far as is possible, be based on the actual flow of goods. Thus, actual cost is seen as the ideal measure but if that is not practical then the best approximation, often taken to be FIFO or average cost, should be used. LIFO is not considered to be a close enough approximation.

Of course there are examples where LIFO does reflect the actual flow of goods. For example, consider an inventory consisting of goods stored in a bin. When goods are sold they are taken from the top of the bin and hence are, unless someone has stirred the bin, those which were most recently acquired. However, the advocates of LIFO do not base their case on the way in which goods are stored. Their argument is that LIFO gives the best approximation to the current value of the 'cost of goods sold' that can be achieved within the historical cost system.

LOWER OF COST OR MARKET VALUE

An asset is such only in so far as it represents a store of future benefits to its owner. If the market value of the inventory falls below cost then it is argued that the inventory should be written down to its market value. A simple enough statement but it does beg a number of questions. What is market value? How is it found?

Two interpretations of market value are available; the price which the firm would currently have to pay in order to acquire the goods, and the amount which it expects to get from the sale of the goods, i.e. replacement cost and net realizable value (NRV). The latter is defined as the amount the firm would receive from the sale of the goods less the anticipated costs that would have to be incurred in selling them.

Neither of these market values can be determined with complete objectivity, for there are a number of problems, some of which are outlined below.

1. The price paid often depends on the quantity purchased. The usual way of dealing with this is to use the price which applies to the quantity in which the firm normally deals.
2. If the business were forced to sell its inventory all at once it would most probably receive a lower price per unit than if it sold the inventory over a period in the normal course of business. Unless there is evidence to the contrary it is assumed that the firm will be able to sell its goods in the normal course of business (going concern convention) but it is not always easy to decide whether the assumption is a reasonable one.
3. There may not be a clearly identifiable price. This is obviously

true of assets that are unique For example, every secondhand car differs from all others of the same type and age due to differences in usage and condition. Trade guides exist, but the application of the guides necessarily involves the use of personal opinion.

A business which trades in a particular type of merchandise must obviously expect to be able to sell the goods for more than it pays for them. Thus, in general, the net realizable value of inventory will be greater than the replacement cost. So writing down the inventory to its replacement cost will, usually, mean that a lower profit will be reported in the period in which the write-down is made than if the net realizable value had been used. However, the use of replacement cost means that the firm will probably be able to show some profit in the period in which the goods are sold, while the use of net realizable value means that it is likely that there will be no profit to report when the goods are eventually sold.

In the United Kingdom net realizable value is favoured because, if replacement cost were used, the loss recorded would be greater than the one which the firm expects to suffer.

There is yet another problem: should the 'lower of cost or market' rule (known as COMA) be applied to the inventory as a whole, the different types of inventory or on an item by item basis?

Example 7.2

Widgets	Cost		NRV	
	£	£	£	£
Type A	100		120	
Type B	90		50	
Type C	90	280	95	265
Fudgets				
Type 1	60		70	
Type 2	50	110	45	115
		£390		£380

COMA rule applied:
(a) To the total £380 (NRV)

(b) To the different groups

	£	
widgets	265 (NRV)	
fudgets	110 (cost)	£375

(c) On an individual basis

	£	
widgets A	100 (cost)	
B	50 (NRV)	
C	90 (cost)	
fudgets 1	60 (cost)	
2	45 (NRV)	£345

It is usually argued that, where possible, the rule should be applied item by item. When that is not possible the group basis should be used. The argument against applying the rule to the total inventory is that possible losses on some items should not be masked by anticipated profits on other items. This is based on the conservatism convention (and the COMA rule is an application of this convention) which is that possible losses should be recognized but that recognition should not be given to anticipated profits.

While COMA is conservative it is not as objective as historical cost. So here we have a conflict between two strong influences on traditional accounting practice. When these two influences collide, conservatism is usually the easy winner.

A reader of financial statements might expect to see, in the income statement, the charge against profit caused by the application of the rule, but he will usually be disappointed. The writing down is performed by reducing the amount of the closing inventory rather than stating the inventory at cost and showing the write off as a separate expense. However, if the amount is material it will often be shown by way of a note to the financial statements.

The COMA rule is applied to all current assets, i.e. investments held for conversion into cash. The rule is not applied to fixed assets.

Fixed assets are shown at cost less accumulated depreciation, i.e. net book value, even if the net book value is higher than the net realizable value or the replacement cost of the asset. This is permissible so long as the firm can show that it expects to be able to recover the net book value from the future use of the asset. Thus the distinction between fixed and current assets is an important one when deciding the amount at which an asset may be shown in the balance sheet.

EXERCISES

7.1 'The choice of the method used to determine the cost of goods sold is not very important because it makes very little difference in the long run'. Comment.

7.2

1. No opening inventory

	Purchases	Sales (units)
January	10 @ £x	
June		8
December	6 @ £5	

FIFO inventory at the end of December, £36.

Find x.

2. Opening inventory 10 units. Average cost £5 per unit.

Purchases		Sales (units)
January	20 @ £x	
June		12
December	8 @ £10	

Average (perpetual) cost of inventory at the end of December, £206.

Find *x*.

3. No opening inventory.

Purchases		Sales (units)
January	8 @ £5	
June	x @ £4	
December		2

LIFO inventory at the end of December, £76.

Find *x*.

4. No opening inventory.

Purchases		Sales (units)
January	10 @ £x	
June	10 @ £y	
December		8

Average (periodic) inventory at the end of December, £54.

LIFO inventory at the end of December, £50.

Find *x* and *y*.

7.3 J. Town's inventory at 1 January 19X5 consisted of 100 units, costed as follows:

LIFO	60 units @ £6 (19X4 layer)	360
	40 units @ £4 (19X3 layer)	160
		£520
FIFO	100 units @ £6	£600
Average cost 100 units @ £5·50		£550

During the year ended 31 December 19X5 Town made the following sales and purchases:

Purchases		Sales (units)
January	10 @ £6	
March		40
April	80 @ £10	
June		30
November		20
December	10 @ £12	

State Town's inventory at 31 December 19X5 and the cost of goods sold for the year ended 31 December 19X5 based on:

(a) FIFO   (b) LIFO   (c) average cost (perpetual)

7.4 Roy had an inventory of 1,000 widgets on 1 January 19X4. The 'book value' of his inventory at that date was:

FIFO   £4,000
LIFO   £3,000 (Roy started business in 19X3 so
                  there is only one LIFO layer).

Compare the FIFO and LIFO profits in 19X4 given the following, alternative, scenarios:

	Prices	Physical volume of inventory
1.	Increasing	Increasing
2.	Increasing	Decreasing
3.	Decreasing	Decreasing
4.	Decreasing	Increasing

Illustrate your answers by means of numerical examples.

8 | *Discounts, Control Accounts and Bank Reconciliations*

After our journeyings to the dizzy height of accounting theory we need now to descend to the flatter plains of accounting practice. In this chapter we will deal with a potpourri of practical points: the treatment of discounts, control accounts and bank reconciliations.

DISCOUNTS

In this section we shall deal with 'cash discounts', rather than 'trade discounts'. So we should first dispose of trade discounts.

A manufacturer may maintain a catalogue showing the prices which he recommends should be charged to the final consumer. But clearly he will charge a lower price to wholesalers and retailers. This lower price might be quoted as, say, £100 less 30 per cent discount (i.e. £70), the 30 per cent being termed the trade discount.

This is only another way of expressing the price; the manufacturer will treat the sale as being at £70 and the customer will treat the purchase as costing £70. So the trade discount will not appear in the accounts of either the buyer or the seller.

Cash Discounts

A cash discount is an encouragement to the customer to pay his debts quickly. For example, if A sells B goods for £100 he will send B an invoice for £100; he might add that he will grant a discount of, say, 2 per cent if payment is made within, say, seven days. In outline the way in which cash discounts are recorded is as follows:

When the sale is made it is recorded at its gross amount, i.e.

	£	£
Debtor	100	
Sales		100

If the customer takes advantage of the discount he will only pay £98 and the balance on his account will have to be cleared by a transfer to an account which is usually called the discounts allowed account. The entry is:

	£	£
Cash	98	
Discounts allowed	2	
Debtor		100

The same method is used in the books of the purchaser and the accounting entries would be:

	£	£
On purchase: Inventory (or fixed assets, etc.)	100	
Creditor		100
On the payment of cash:		
Creditor	100	
Cash		98
Discount received		2

Discounts and Books of Prime Entry

Since discounts received and allowed are recorded at the same time as the associated payments and receipts, it is sensible to use the cash book as the book of prime entry, giving it two extra columns as shown in Figure 8.1.

Figure 8.1

Cash Book

	Discounts allowed	Receipts	Discounts received	Payments
B	2	98		

When a net payment is received, it is entered in the cash received column and the discount put into the discount allowed column.

When posting from the cash book to the ledger, the individual items in the discounts allowed column are posted to the credit of the debtors' accounts* and the total of the column is debited to the discounts allowed account.

Similarly the amounts in the discounts received column are individually posted to the debit of the creditors' accounts, while the total is posted to the credit of the discounts received account.

How Should Discounts be Shown in the Income Statement?

There are two conflicting views. The first, which tends to be favoured in the United States, is that discounts allowed should be shown as a deduction from sales revenue while discounts received should be deducted from the cost of whatever was purchased, inventories or fixed assets.

The alternative, which is the one generally adopted in the United Kingdom, is to treat discounts allowed and discounts received as an expense and revenue in their own right. It is argued that these items relate more closely to the financial activities of a business rather than to the trading activities. If, for example, a firm pays its debts quickly in order to obtain cash discounts, the advantage gained may be offset by extra interest paid on its bank overdraft. Thus discounts received and allowed are credited and charged to the profit and loss section of the income statement rather than the trading account (see Chapter 9).

Cash Discounts and Year-end Adjustments

If a firm allows cash discounts, it should consider whether to provide for the discount that it expects to have to grant to its year-end debtors.

The argument for making a provision is that if one were not made the value of the debtors would be overstated. The counter-argument which follows the financial expense line is that the discount is granted to encourage early payment; so the expense should be recognized in the period in which the business received the benefit of the quick payment. In other words, no provision is necessary since the expense should be recognized in the period in which the early payment is received rather than the period in which the sale was made.

Similar considerations apply when deciding whether provision should be made for discounts which the business expects to receive when paying the year-end creditors.

CONTROL ACCOUNTS AND SUBSIDIARY LEDGERS

We have shown how sales made on credit are recorded by debiting the account of the customer and crediting the sales account, while purchases on credit are recorded by debiting the inventory account and crediting the account of the supplier.

* But see the section on Control Accounts.

This would be fine if there were only a few customers and suppliers (as in our convenient examples) but even the smallest business may have a surprisingly large number of credit customers and/or suppliers. So we are going to describe a method whereby the practical problem arising from having a large number of suppliers' and customers' accounts (or personal accounts) can be dealt with. The method yields a bonus in that it can help in exercising a degree of 'internal control' over the operation of the business.

The important topic of internal control is outside the scope of this book but in passing we should mention that it is concerned, among other things, with establishing systems that ensure that the firm's assets are safeguarded and that its transactions are properly authorized. However, the aspect of internal control which concerns us here is the maintenance of accurate and reliable records in the form of the books of account of the firm by guarding against error and fraud.

The Problems Caused by Having Numerous Personal Accounts

Let us consider the main problems caused by having a large number of ledger accounts.

1. Locating errors will be difficult, tedious and time-consuming. In particular, if the trial balance fails to balance, the postings to many hundreds of ledger accounts, the casts of the accounts and the extraction of the balances will have to be checked. We shall return to this point later.
2. The existence of a large number of accounts implies that a lot of book-keeping is required. But if the ledger accounts are all in one place it is impossible for more than one book-keeper to use the ledger at the same time.

A sensible way of dealing with the second problem is physically to split the ledger. A logical way of doing this is to put all the customers' accounts into a *debtors' ledger* and all the suppliers' accounts into a *creditors' ledger* leaving the other accounts in the original ledger. The first two ledgers are often called the *personal ledgers* while the remainder of the original ledger is called the *general* or *nominal ledger.* Sometimes the general ledger is further subdivided by forming a ledger called the *private ledger*, containing those accounts which management may not wish to be open to inspection by the common herd of book-keepers. The private ledger might, in a limited company, contain the accounts for directors' remuneration and so on.

This division allows more people to work on the ledger at the same time, but it does not help us to locate errors more easily or to exercise any internal control. The next step is to replace all the debtors' accounts that we have removed from the ledger by a single account called the debtors' control account and all the creditors' accounts by a creditors' control account.

This means that the debtors' and creditors' ledgers have been removed from the double-entry system, becoming what may be called subsidiary ledgers, and the personal accounts contained therein similarly become memorandum accounts.

The Mechanics

Before dealing with the advantages of control accounts we must describe their mechanics.

Suppose that postings from the daybooks to the ledger are made monthly. Then, each month, postings would be made to the personal accounts as before, but additionally the total of the individual postings would be posted to the control account. Take the debtors' control account as an example, the control account would be debited with the total sales for the month and credited with the monthly totals of:

cash received
discounts allowed
sales returns, and
bad debts written off.

If all this is done properly, the balance on the control account will equal the total of the balances of the accounts controlled by it. This process is illustrated in Figure 8.2. Note that the opening balance on the control account, £220, is equal to the total of the balances on the individual accounts, i.e.

	£
A	90
B	80
C	50
	£220

Since the total of the individual sales and cash postings has been made to the control account, this equality also holds after the postings have been made. For the closing balance on the control account (not shown in Figure 8.2) is £680 while the balances on the personal accounts are:

	£
A	100
B	200
C	380
	£680

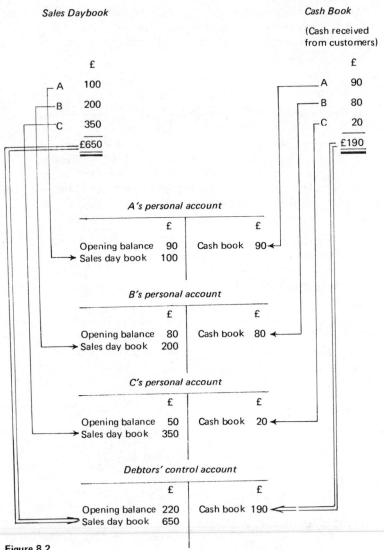

Figure 8.2

Some of our readers may be getting disturbed, fearing that after struggling with double-entry book-keeping they will now have to start learning treble-entry book-keeping. We are happy to be able to say that this is not the case, for remember that the introduction of the control accounts has relegated the personal accounts to the status of memorandum accounts which are *outside the double-entry system.*

The double entry is completed, using the above example,

by	Debiting	Debtors' control account
	Crediting	Sales account
and	Debiting	Cash account
	Crediting	Debtors' control account

The postings which form part of the double-entry system have been indicated in Figure 8.2 by the double lines.

However, despite the adherence to the double-entry system it is clear that the use of control accounts will necessitate a modification in the use of the daybooks in that, as well as showing the double-entry postings, they must also give the instructions to post to the personal (memorandum) accounts. Example 8.1 provides greater detail.

Example 8.1

Daybooks and extracts from daybooks

Sales Daybook

Date		Invoice No.	Memo posting	£
	Alpha Limited		A1	500
	Beta Limited		B1	300
	Gamma Limited		G1	120
				£920

Double-entry posting

			£
Debit	Debtors' control account D1		920
Credit	Sales account S1		920

Purchases Daybook

Date		Invoice No.	Memo posting	£
	Exe Limited		E1	300
	Why Limited		W1	200
	Gamma Limited		G2	80
				£580

Double-entry posting

			£
Debit	Inventory account I1		580
Credit	Creditors' control account C1		580

Extract from Cash Book

(a) Receipts Side

	Memo posting	Discounts allowed £	Cash received £
Alpha Limited	A1	8	392
Beta Limited	B1	4	196
		£12	£588

Double-entry postings

			£
Discounts:	Debit	Discounts allowed account D2	12
	Credit	Debtors' control account D1	12
Cash:	Credit	Debtors' control account D1 (The entry in the cash book serves as the debit entry)	588

(b) Payments side

	Memo posting	Discounts received £	Cash paid £
Exe Limited	E1	15	485
Why Limited	W1	—	100
		£15	£585

Double-entry postings

			£
Discounts:	Debit	Creditors' control account D1	15
	Credit	Discounts' received account D3	15
Cash:	Debit	Creditors' control account C1 (The entry in the cash book serves as the credit entry)	585

Extract from Journal

Date		Fo.	£	£
	Provision against Doubtful debts			
	account	P1	150	
	Debtors control account	D1		150
	Being bad debts written off			
	Memo posting:			
	Delta Limited	D4		150
	Creditors' control account	C1	60	
	Inventory account	I1		60
	Being the cost of goods returned			
	to Exe Limited			
	Memo posting:			
	Exe Limited	E1	60	
	Creditors' control account	C1	100	
	Debtors' control account	D1		100
	Being the setting off of Gamma's			
	Creditors' personal account against			
	the balance on Gamma's Debtors'			
	personal account.			
	Memo postings:			
	Gamma Limited	G2	100	
	Gamma Limited	G1		100

1. The firm might use a purchases return daybook and/or a purchases return account especially if there are a significant number of purchases returns.
2. Gamma Limited is both a customer and supplier of the firm and it has been agreed that the balance on his creditors personal account can be set off against the balance on his debtors personal account.

Location of Errors

Suppose that a firm has 40 nominal ledger accounts, 400 debtors' personal accounts and 250 creditors' personal accounts. Further suppose that in the posting of cash received of £513 from a customer to the credit of his account the figures 1 and 3 are transposed, i.e. £531 is credited instead of £513. We should find that the trial balance does not balance, but without control accounts we should have no idea where to start looking for the error. We should have to check all the additions in all the daybooks and the posting to, the additions of and the extraction of balances of all 690 ledger accounts. A formidable task.

If control accounts are used then, so long as the total cash received from customers has been correctly cast and posted, the trial balance will balance, since the personal accounts no longer form part of the double-entry system. We should find that the balance on the debtors control account does not equal the total of the balances on the personal accounts because one of them is wrong. There is still some work to do, but at least we would know where to start looking for the error.

Now suppose that the error was in one of the nominal ledger accounts. The trial balance would not balance but since the control accounts balance (i.e. the balance on the control accounts agrees with the total of the balances of the accounts controlled by them) we know that we should confine our attention to the nominal ledger accounts.

Control Accounts and Internal Control

A basic feature of a system of internal control is that one or more people should be able to check the work of others. Control accounts provide a good example of this.

The person or department responsible for the nominal ledger is provided with the information needed to complete the double entry and will be able to determine the balances on the control accounts. They are thus able to check, on a day to day basis, the work of the departments responsible for keeping the personal accounts.

BANK RECONCILIATION STATEMENTS

The purpose of these statements is to explain the difference between the balance on the ledger account recording the firm's balance at bank ('cash account') and the balance shown on the firm's bank statement. In general, for the reasons given below, these will differ.

Bank Statements

Bank statements often cause considerable confusion to double-entry novices since they appear to be the wrong way round — payments are debited while receipts are credited. The reason is that a bank statement is a copy of the customer's account in the books of the bank. So when the customer pays something into the bank his asset is increased but the bank's liability to the customer is increased. This is why 'credit balance' is used to describe what is, from the point of view of the customer, an asset and hence a debit balance.

Differences Between the Cash Book and Bank Statement

These are caused by errors and timing differences. Once upon a time any errors were likely to be made by the customer but nowadays banks, for various reasons, are likely to invent some interesting errors of their own. Errors made by the customer are corrected in his books and will not appear in the bank reconciliation. Errors made by the bank will appear in the bank reconciliation statement until the bank eventually accedes to the pleas of the anguished customer and corrects them.

The most common timing difference is due to unpresented cheques. These are cheques which have been issued by the firm and hence have been recorded in its cash book but which have not, at the date of the bank reconciliation, reached its bank.

There will usually be a good number of unpresented cheques at any time because a cheque has a long road to travel and its journey can easily take up to seven working days even if everyone concerned (including the post office) is reasonably efficient. A cheque's peregrination is shown in Figure 8.3.

Other timing differences are due to cash and cheques banked by the customer which have not reached his bank statement. The delay may be due to the receipts being banked other than at the customer's branch of the bank or because the receipts were paid in on the day that the bank statement was prepared. If a firm's customers make use of the bank Giro system which means, in effect, that they pay directly into the firm's bank account, the firm may not be aware of the amount of its receipts until it receives its bank statement. In this case the firm should record the receipts in its books in the normal way and hence no entry need be made in the bank reconciliation statement.

Figure 8.3

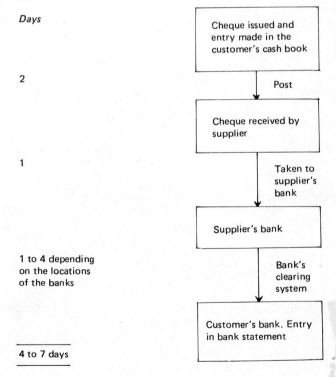

The Outline of a Bank Reconciliation Statement

The procedure for preparing a bank reconciliation statement is as follows:

1. It is usual to start with the balance as shown on the bank statement. (It will be assumed that the account is not in overdraft.)
2. To this is added cash and cheques received which have been entered into the cash book which have not yet found their way to the bank statement. These items are sometimes collectively called 'lodgements not yet credited'.
3. 'Cheques not yet presented' are then deducted. As explained above, these are cheques which have been issued by the firm but which have yet to be entered on the bank statement.
4. Errors made by the bank will be added or subtracted depending on their nature.

Once these steps are completed, the result should be the balance in the cash book.

Example 8.2

The following details relate to B.L. Link.

Cash Book
for the month of March 19X3

		£			£
1 Mar	Balance	2,100	3 Mar	Splodd	200 ✓
10 Mar	Bank Giro		10 Mar	Muncher	8
	transfer	70 ✓	12 Mar	Clodd	18 ✓
15 Mar	Fidget	180 ✓	12 Mar	Ofe	700 ✓
31 Mar	Crunn	1,100	16 Mar	Thykk	97 ✓
			23 Mar	Blank	600
		3,450			1,623

Bank Reconciliation Statement at 28 February 19X3

	£
Balance per bank statement	2,250
less Cheque not yet presented:	
Putt	150
Balance per cash book	£2,100

Bank Statement

Date	Particulars	Payments	Receipts	Balance
		£	£	£
19X5				
1 Mar	Opening balance			2,250
4 Mar	Splodd	200√		2,050
6 Mar	Putt	150√		1,900
10 Mar	Bank Giro transfer		70√	1,970
14 Mar	Clodd	18√		1,952
17 Mar	Fidget		180√	2,132
19 Mar	Soho Entertainments Ltd	200		1,932
20 Mar	Thykk	97√		1,835
21 Mar	Ofe	700√		1,135
24 Mar	Trade Association (standing order)	* 10		1,125
28 Mar	Bank charges	* 28		1,097
31 Mar	Bank Giro transfer		* 500	1,597

Step 1

The bank statement is checked against the cash book. The sign √ has been used to indicate the items which appear in both places. Note that Putt's cheque had appeared in the cash book prior to 1 March and hence appeared in the bank reconciliation statement as at 28 February.

Step 2

Of the four items that appear in the bank statement but not in the cash book, three should be entered in the cash book (these have been indicated by *). The cheque payable to Soho Entertainments was in fact not drawn by B. L. Link but by the Rev. L. B. Link and should have been debited to his account.

Accordingly the entries shown below are made in the cash book:

Cash Book

	£		£
Total from above	3,450	Total from above	1,623
Bank Giro transfer	500	Subscriptions to trade association	10
		Bank charges	28
		Balance c/d	2,289
	£3,950		£3,950
Balance b/d	2,289		

Step 3

The remaining unticked items, i.e., those items which are in the cash book but not the bank statement, and vice versa, appear on the bank reconciliation statement.

Bank Reconciliation Statement
as at 31 March 19X3

	£	£
Balance per bank statement		1,597
add Lodgement not yet credited		
— Crun	1,100	
Bank error — cheque debited		
in error	200	1,300
		2,897
less Cheques not yet presented		
—Muncher	8	
— Blank	600	608
Balance per cash book		£2,289

EXERCISES

8.1 The following information relates to the activities of F. Head, a trader, for the year ended 30 June 19X6.

Bad debts written off £150. Purchases £48,200.
Cash received from customers £58,000. Purchase returns £400.
Cash paid to suppliers £49,000. Sales £61,500.
Discounts allowed £600. Sales returns £1,100.
Discounts received £420.

At 1 July 19X5 Head's trade creditors amounted to £3,400 and his trade debtors to £4,600.

Draw up F. Head's debtors' and creditors' control accounts for the year ended 30 June 19X6.

8.2 The balance on J. Alp's creditors' account as at 31 December 19X2 was £11,113. A list of the balances on the creditors' ledger as at that date revealed the following:

	£	£
Sundry credit balances		10,204
less Debit balances		
Sol's account	45	
Lui's account	300	345
		£9,859

During your investigations you discover the following:

1. The purchase daybook has been undercast by £70.

2. A purchase of £500 from Tun had not been posted to his personal account.

3. The debit balance on Sol's account was caused by the error of posting a payment to Sol's account as £94 instead of £49.

4. The debit balance on Lui's account represents a payment in advance demanded by Lui.

5. Discounts received amounting to £691 had been posted to the personal accounts but not to the control account.

6. A bad debt of £65 written off Lee's personal account in the debtors' ledger has been posted to the creditors' control account.

7. An invoice for £820 rendered by Dai had been badly typed and Alp's book-keeper had read it as £520.

8. A contra entry of £23 between Tol's accounts in the debtors' and creditors' ledgers had been correctly entered in the personal accounts but had not been entered in the control accounts.

(a) Show the necessary correcting journal entries.

(b) Show the revised control account balance and the adjustments to the list of balances, showing that, after correction, the control account balance and the list of balances are in agreement.

(c) The correct balance on the debtors' control account is £17,125 (no accounts in the debtors' ledger have credit balances). What amounts should be shown in the balance sheet for trade debtors and trade creditors?

8.3 The book-keeper of H. Smith has a problem — the debtors' ledger does not balance.

The balance on the debtors' control accounts is £3,054 but the following list of balances has been extracted from the debtors' ledger:

	£
A	1,076
B	422
C	869
D	1,331
	£3,698

The various ledger accounts are given below.

Debtors' Control Account

Opening balance	1,200	Cash	7,628
Sales	9,179	Sales returns	48
Bad debts expense		Discounts received	52
— bad debts written off	192		
— increase in provision	211		

A

Opening balance	650	Cash	3,700
Sales	4,210	Discounts allowed	84

B

Opening balance	150	Cash	2,817
Sales	3,158	Sales returns	48
		Discounts allowed	21

C

Opening balance	70	Cash	973
Sales	1,811	Discounts allowed	12

D

Opening balance	138	Cash	138
Sales	1,331		

E

Opening balance	192	Bad debts	192

Redraft the ledger accounts, where necessary, eliminating the errors and show that the debtors' ledger can be balanced. If it is not clear which of two figures is the correct one, assume that the figure given in the personal account is correct.

8.4 The balance as at 30 June 19X6, on the cash book of Jim France was a credit of £947.

An examination of the cash book and bank statements revealed the following:

1. A cheque drawn in favour of France by Holland for £260 had been dishonoured. No entry regarding the dishonour had been made in the cash book.

2. Cheques amounting to £1,570 had been issued by France before 30 June, but had not been presented by that date.

3. £650 receipts from customers had been credited to France's bank account through the bank Giro system but no entry had been made in the cash book.

4. France paid cheques amounting to £724 into a branch of his bank on the morning of 30 June but this deposit had not been recorded in the bank statement.

5. The bank had 'credited' France's account with a receipt of £42 which should have been credited to the account of his brother, A. France.

6. The total of the payments side of France's cash book at the foot of page 17 was £12,175 which had been carried to the top of page 18 as £12,715.

7. Bank charges and interest of £76 had been charged by the bank but had not been entered in the cash book.

8. France had purchased a subscription for an American trade magazine. The bank had made this payment on France's behalf. France had estimated that the sterling cost of the subscription was £12 and had shown it in the cash book as such. The bank statement recorded that the cost had actually been £14.

(a) Make the appropriate adjustments in the cash book showing the correct balance.

(b) Prepare the bank reconciliation statement as at 30 June 19X6.

8.5 A. S. Brown's cash book and bank statement for the month of September 19X9 are given below. Prepare Brown's bank reconciliation statement as at 30 September 19X9.

Note Brown did not issue a cheque numbered 342

Cash Book

		£				Cheque No.	£
Sept 1	Balance	111	Sept 1	Smith		931	1,434
8	Sundry receipts	1,200	3	Jones		932	2,477
12	" "	850	4	Hayes		933	357
15	" "	920	5	Curry		934	20
18	" "	1,017	6	Bulgaria		935	4
18	" "	221	7	Wellington		936	368
25	" "	500	12	Cholet		937	101
30	" "	452	14	Bungo		938	31
		5,271	20	Tobermory		939	14
			22	Dougal		940	1,218
			23	Florence		941	99
			26	Dylan		942	99
			27	Zebedee		943	99
							6,321

Bank Statement

Date	Particulars	Payments	Receipts	Balance
Sept 1	Opening balance			691
1	Sundry credit		860	1,551
1	926	1,010		541
5	931	1,434		893 O.D.
6	932	2,477		3,370 O.D.
7	929	430		3,800 O.D.
8	Sundry credit		1,200	2,600 O.D.
10	934	20		2,620 O.D.
10	935	4		2,624 O.D.
11	933	357		2,981 O.D.
12	Sundry credit		850	2,131 O.D.
15	Sundry credit		920	1,211 O.D.
15	342	280		1,491 O.D.
18	Sundry credit		1,238	253 O.D.
19	938	31		284 O.D.
25	Sundry credit		500	216
27	Bank Giro		480	696
28	940	1,218		522 O.D.
29	Charges	40		562 O.D.
30	939	14		576 OD.
30	941	99		675 O.D.
30	936	368		1,043 O.D.

9 | *Presentation of Financial Statements*

The financial statements consist essentially of the income statement (or profit and loss account) and the balance sheet. This package is sometimes called the 'final accounts' as it has to be produced at the end of each accounting year. However, interim financial statements are very often produced and in such cases the use of the phrase 'final accounts' is misleading.

We have dealt with financial statements *ad nauseam* but have not hitherto discussed how they are (or should be) presented. So we shall now concentrate on the words and the arrangement of the figures rather than the figures themselves. Why is this topic important? The reason can be conveniently analysed under three heads.

1. *Highlighting significant figures and relationships.* Financial statements are part of the communications process whereby the accountant transmits certain selected information about the business to the readers of the financial statements; the way the information is presented can be almost as important as the information itself. For example, the balance sheet could correctly (in a numerical sense) be presented as a list of *n* assets, with the fixed assets mixed up with the current assets; and a list of *m* credit balances, beautifully confusing liabilities and owners' equity items. An example of such a presentation is shown on pages 129–130. Now the informed reader of the accounts could pick out the salient points, though to do so would probably have to redraft the balance sheet. But what about the not-so-well-informed reader? In all probability, he would be completely and utterly lost. Therefore we should ensure that the financial statements are designed in such a way as to save informed readers some work and provide a gleam of light for the uninformed.

2. *Convenience.* This is much less important than the first reason, but it can be of help. It may be of no significance whether A comes

before B or B before A. But if most accountants always put A
before B then readers will become used to it and this will help
them when looking for A and B.

3. *The law.* There is no legal 'guidance' as to the way which the
accounts of a sole trader should be presented. Indeed there is no
legal requirement for a sole trader to produce financial statements
at all. However, the law does take more than a passing interest in
the accounts of limited liability companies (as well as some other
forms of company). For example, the Companies Act 1967
specifies, so far as balance sheets are concerned, that 'fixed assets,
current assets and assets that are neither fixed nor current shall be
separately identified'.*

Although the provisions of the Companies Act do not extend to sole
traders, accountants often apply them, where appropriate, to the financial
statements of sole traders, basically for the reasons given above.

THE BALANCE SHEET

Assets, liabilities and owners' equity are the three fundamental components
of the balance sheet. The primary effect of any presentation, therefore, must
be to clarify these main groups.

Assets

We have already identified two sorts of assets, fixed and current assets†
and the balance sheet should tell readers which sort each asset is. This
is particularly important because the distinction depends on the use to
which management intends to put an asset rather than the nature of the
asset; or the reader could not, in some cases, make the distinction himself.

The totals of the fixed and current assets are important; so these
totals (or rather sub-totals, to distinguish them from the grand totals of
assets, etc.) should be shown.

There is no statutory order for marshalling the items under the headings of fixed or current assets. In the United Kingdom, it is the convention
to list the assets in order of permanence, e.g. freehold property before
motor vehicles under fixed assets, and inventory before cash under current
assets.

Contra Asset Accounts

We have already introduced contra asset accounts (i.e. accumulated

---

* Companies Act, 1967. Schedule 2 paragraph 4 (2).
† We will not deal with those assets which are neither fixed nor current (for which no
generally agreed collective noun exists) at this time but the same principles apply.

depreciation and provision against doubtful debts) in Chapter 6. The accumulated depreciation shows the amount of the cost of the asset which has to date been converted into an expense. However, the cost of the fixed asset is a relevant figure; so we maintain two accounts, the cost of the asset and the accumulated depreciation. We carry forward this separation into the balance sheet and show both balances, and as these figures are so closely related we place them together. One way of doing so is illustrated below.

Fixed assets	*Cost*	*Accumulated depreciation*	*Net book value*
	£	£	£
Freehold property	50,000	—	50,000
Fixtures and fittings	14,000	8,000	6,000
Motor vehicles	8,000	5,000	3,000
	£72,000	£13,000	£59,000

The same principle applies to the provision against doubtful debts: its balance should be set off against the debtors' figure. The only difference is that if the provision is 'not material' only the net amount is shown.

Liabilities

The usual definition of a current liability is that it is a liability which must be discharged within a year of the date of the balance sheet. The total of the current liabilities is therefore a very important figure, since it gives an indication of the cash that the firm will have to find in the short run, hence, it is separated from longer-term liabilities. The Companies Act goes further, distinguishing between liabilities which are payable within five years of the balance sheet date and longer-term liabilities.

THE DESIGN OF THE BALANCE SHEET

We shall assume that a business had fixed and current assets, current liabilities and long-term liabilities and, of course, owners' equity.

The 'Horizontal' Balance Sheet

The distinguishing feature of the horizontal balance sheet is that it has two sides. One way of presenting a horizontal balance sheet is as follows:

	£		£
Owners' equity	x	Fixed assets	x
Long-term liabilities	x	Current assets	x
Current liabilities	x		
	£x		£x

It is considered 'good form' to write the two balance sheet totals on the same line.

One strange feature of the British way of presenting the horizontal balance sheet is that the credit balances (owners' equity and creditors) are on the left-hand side which is, you will remember, reserved for debit balances. So the British balance sheet is the wrong way round. In the United States, a more consistent approach is adopted and the assets appear on the left.

The 'Vertical' Balance Sheet

If all that is too complicated, then we could arrange a balance sheet so that one 'side' is put above rather than next to the other 'side'. This form of presentation is known as a vertical balance sheet. One way of designing a vertical balance sheet is shown below.

	£	£
Fixed assets		x
Current assets	x	
less: Current liabilities	x	x
		£x
Representing:		
Owners' equity		x
Long-term liabilities		x
		£x

There are a number of variations on the above theme; for example, the owners' equity and long-term liabilities section could be put first.

Working Capital

Notice that in the above form the total of the current liabilities has been deducted from the current assets. The difference between the current assets and current liabilities is known as 'working capital' or 'net current assets'. This is an important figure, and it should be disclosed. Why is it important?

1. Current assets consist of cash and those assets which will be converted into cash within a relatively short time, usually a year.

Strictly, current assets are those assets which will be converted into cash within one year of the balance sheet date or within the operating cycle if that is longer than one year. The operating cycle can be described as the time it takes the business to acquire (or manufacture) the goods, sell them and collect the cash. For most trading companies, a year is the effective criterion used to define current assets. Current liabilities are those liabilities which have to be discharged, again, within a year or the operating cycle if longer. So the difference between these two totals gives some indication of the short-term financial strength of the business, i.e. the likelihood that it will be able to pay off short-term creditors without disrupting the business (by selling some of the fixed assets, for instance) or obtaining additional finance. In that sense, the more the current assets exceed the current liabilities the better.

2. In order to operate, a business must (in general) invest in fixed assets but it must also invest in current assets. A trading company must hold some inventory and in most trades sales are made on credit so it must also have some debtors. Now some of that type of investment may be 'self-financed' in that, for example, inventories are purchased on credit. Generally, however, the business will have to make its own investment in current assets. Thus the presentation of the working capital figure is valuable, because it shows the investment which the firm must itself make in current assets. Looked at this way, a high working capital figure may not be a good thing, since it might represent excessive investment in current assets, e.g. the business may be carrying an excessively high inventory. This point should be contrasted with point 1 above.

Bank overdrafts (as distinguished from bank loans) present a problem in that they are really current liabilities: the banker can call for repayment on demand. However, in many cases he would not dream of doing so, since he, and his client, consider the overdraft to be a medium-term (say two or three years), rather than a short-term, form of finance. In fact many firms operate very successfully on an overdraft for years, and in these cases it is clear that they are treated as long-term sources of finance. In such cases the inclusion of bank overdrafts under current liabilities on a balance sheet would arguably distort the working capital figure.

Notice that in the above outline the total of long-term liabilities and owners' equity has been presented, thus highlighting the long-term sources of finance.

The vertical form of balance sheet, which we prefer, is a good example of how the intelligent design of the balance sheet can help the user of the accounts to pick out some of the significant figures. Example 9.1 gives an extended illustration of the horizontal and vertical forms of balance sheet (see pages 130–134).

THE INCOME STATEMENT (OR PROFIT AND LOSS ACCOUNT)

The Trading Account

Essentially the income statement for a period consists of the revenue for the period less the expenses deemed to have been incurred in earning that revenue.

There is one type of expense which is considered to be so important that it is given special treatment — the cost of goods sold. Suppose we wanted to examine the profit earned by a retailer. It would often be convenient to start by looking at two aspects:

> the difference between the amount for which the goods were sold and the cost of the goods (known as mark-up); and
> the overheads (wages, rent, etc.) which were incurred in selling the goods and running the business.

We might find two companies whose profits, expressed as a percentage of sales, are the same, but observe that one has a high mark-up and high overheads (e.g. a small specialist shop) while the other has a low mark-up and low overheads (e.g. a discount store). Similarly, if a businessman believes that his profit is too low, one of the first things he should do is to look at the mark-up and overheads and see whether one, or both, has got out of control.

The cost of goods sold is given special treatment in the form of a trading account (which is a section of the income statement). A trading account may appear as follows:

	£
Sales	100,000
less Cost of goods sold	60,000
Gross profit	£40,000

But often, especially in the United Kingdom, more detail is given about the cost of goods sold, thus:

	£	£
Sales		100,000
less Opening stock (or inventory)	35,000	
Purchases	70,000	
	105,000	
less Closing stock (or inventory)	45,000	60,000
Gross profit (40%)		40,000

The expenses which are charged to the trading account are those which have been incurred in getting the goods to the point of sale. These could include carriage inwards, import duties, etc., if they have been charged separately from the cost of the goods themselves.

The gross profit (or margin in the United States) is the difference between the sales and the cost of goods sold. The gross profit is often expressed as a percentage of sales and may be displayed in the trading account as shown above.

Horizontal and Vertical Income Statements

Like the balance sheet the income statement can be produced in a horizontal or vertical form. The horizontal form, which is going out of fashion, is as follows:

Income Statement

(*or Trading and Profit and Loss Account*)

for the period ended 31 December 19X4

	£		£
Opening stock	x	Sales	x
Purchases	x		
	x		
less Closing stock	x		
Cost of goods sold	x		
Gross profit, carried down	x		
	$£x$		$£x$
		Gross profit, brought down	x
Expenses			
Wages	x		
etc.	x		
etc.	x		
	x		
Net profit	x		
	$£x$		$£x$

The vertical form of income statement is shown below:

Income Statement

(*or Trading and Profit and Loss Account*)

for the period ended 31 December 19X4

	£	£
Sales		x
less Opening stock	x	
Purchases	x	
	x	
less Closing stock	x	x
Gross profit		x
less Expenses	x	
	x	
	x	x
Net profit		£x

The list of expenses will often be long, and the user of the accounts may find it difficult to appreciate properly the information given if he is simply presented with a list of, say, 25 phrases and figures. Thus it is good practice to classify the expense items under appropriate headings and show the totals of the various classes. This approach is illustrated in Example 9.1.

There is no laid down scheme for classification and, indeed, the way in which expense items are classified should depend on the nature of the business. However, the classification used in the example, i.e. classifying expenses under the headings of administrative, selling and distribution, and financial expenses, is quite widely used.

Manufacturing and Appropriation Accounts

The outline income statements presented above will suffice for a sole trader. The income statement comprises two parts, the trading account and the profit and loss account. However, the 'profit and loss account' is also very often used as a synonym for the whole of the income statement.

If the business is a manufacturing one, however, it is necessary to add a manufacturing account which shows the cost of goods produced during the period. The cost of goods produced is carried down to the trading account where it replaces (or supplements) the purchases figure.

If we are concerned with an entity which has more than one owner –

a partnership or a limited company, it will be necessary to show how the profit (or loss) for the period has been divided. The statement which shows how this is done is termed the appropriation account.

So the complete 'package' incorporated in the income statement includes:

Manufacturing account
Trading account
Profit and loss account
Appropriation account

COMPARATIVE FIGURES

A figure in isolation is usually meaningless. We must have a yardstick against which we can judge the figure. The yardstick may be an intuitive one which enables one to say something like 'on the basis of what I know about the circumstances in which the business found itself last year the wages were too high'.

There are more objective yardsticks available, such as the average figures for firms in the same business. There is one yardstick which (except in the first year of a firm's life) is always available – last year's figures. These comparative figures are often shown on both the income statement and the balance sheet, and indeed the Companies Acts require limited companies to show comparatives (last year's figures) in the published accounting statements.

There is one danger about the use of comparatives: it is easy to draw naïve conclusions. Suppose a firm's sales and profits are both very much higher than last year. A naïve conclusion is that the firm has done well but, of course, all we can really say is that it has done better, for its performance last year may have been absymal while this year it may have been merely awful.

Example 9.1

FRED

Balance Sheet

Item			*Item*		
1.	Provision against doubtful debts	400	9.	Inventory	80,000
2.	Electricity payable	200	10.	Cash in hand	5
3.	Capital account	228,605	11.	Freehold property,	
4.	Motor vehicle, depreciation	14,000		at cost	150,000
5.	Trade creditors	58,000	12.	Rates prepaid	1,000
6.	Wages payable	2,000	13.	Motor vehicles, at	
7.	Long-term loan	40,000		cost	20,000
8.	Long-term loan interest	500	14.	Trade debtors	90,000
			15.	Balance at bank	2,000
			16.	Insurance prepaid	700
		343,705			343,705

Income Statement

Item			Item		
17.	Rates	8,000	42.	Closing inventory	80,000
18.	Carriage out*	15,000	43.	Sales	600,000
19.	Subscriptions	12			
20.	Depreciation	2,000			680,000
21.	Carriage in*	4,200			
22.	Gas for central heating	200			
23.	Interest on bank loans	300			
24.	Post and stationery	3,000			
25.	Newspapers	25			
26.	Bad debts	705			
27.	Printing	620			
28.	Wages	80,000			
29.	Purchases	420,000			
30.	Sundry expenses	5,000			
31.	Charitable donations	3			
32.	Electricity	4,800			
33.	Interest on loan	4,000			
34.	Advertising	18,000			
35.	Sales returns	400			
36.	Insurance	6,000			
37.	Repairs to typewriter	12			
38.	Opening inventory	70,000			
39.	Employer's contribution to National Insurance	5,000			
40.	Travelling expenses	2,500			
41.	Net profit	30,223			
		680,000			

*Carriage out is the cost of sending goods to customers. Carriage in is the cost which the firm has to pay to have goods delivered to itself.

The above are not very helpful. The financial statements, after redesign and correction are shown below:

Notes	Vertical Form

FRED

(a)	Balance Sheet as at 31 December 19X4			
(b)		£ Cost	£ Accumulated depreciation	£ Net book value
	Fixed assets			
(c)	Freehold property	150,000	—	150,000
	Motor vehicles	20,000	14,000	6,000
		£170,000	£14,000	£156,000

	Current assets		156,000
(d)	Inventory at the lower of cost and net realizable value	80,000	
(e)	Trade debtors less provision against doubtful debts	89,600	
(f)	Prepaid expenses	1,700	
(g)	Balance at bank and cash in hand	2,005	
		173,305	

	less Current liabilities			
	Trade creditors	58,000		
(h)	Accrued expenses	2,700	60,700	112,605
	Net assets			£268,605

	financed by:	
(i)	*Owners' capital account*	
	Capital at 1 January 19X4	216,382
	Profit for the year	30,223
		246,605
	less Drawings	18,000
		228,605
(j)	Long-term loan repayable 1 January 19XX.	40,000
		£268,605

Notes	Income Statement			
(a)	Year ended 31 December 19X4			
(b)		£	£	£
(k)	Sales			599,600
	less Opening inventory		70,000	
(l)	Purchases and carriage in		424,200	
			494,200	
	less Closing inventory		80,000	414,200
	Gross profit			185,400
	less Administrative expenses			
(m)	Administrative wages	53,000		
	Rates	8,000		
	Insurance	6,000		
(n)	Light and heat	5,000		
(o)	Printing, postage and stationery	3,620		
(p)	Sundry expenses	5,052	80,672	
			80,672	185,400

	Selling and distribution expenses		80,672	185,400
(m)	Salesmens' wages	32,000		
	Carriage out	15,000		
	Advertising	18,000		
	Salesmens' expenses	2,500		
	Bad debts	705		
(q)	Depreciation of motor vehicles	2,000	70,205	
	Financial expenses			
	Interest on long-term loan	4,000		
(r)	Interest on bank loan	300	4,300	155,177
	Net profit			£30,223

Notes

(a)   The date of the balance sheet and the period covered by the income statement should be stated.

(b)   One of the deficiencies of the original statements was that the monetary units were not stated. It is the custom to head the columns with the £ sign and to place the sign before the total figures.

(c)   The use of the word 'depreciation' on the original balance sheet (item 4) was confusing in that it could imply that it was the depreciation expense for the year. A better description is 'accumulated depreciation' or 'depreciation charged to date'. Note the advantages of the method used to show the fixed assets. The contra asset account of accumulated depreciation has been set off against the asset account; the fact that no depreciation has been charged in respect of freehold property has been highlighted; and the totals of the cost of fixed assets, the accumulated depreciation and the net book value are given.

(d)   It is usual to show the basis used in arriving at the inventory figure.

(e)   The provision against doubtful debts (another contra asset account) has been set off against debtors. Since the amount concerned (£400) is not judged significant it has not been disclosed.

(f)   There are a number of reasonably small prepaid expenses (items 12 and 16) and these have been combined.

(g)   The cash in hand is only £5 and there seems little point in showing it separately.

(h)   As (f). Items 2, 6 and 8 make up this figure.

(i)   In the original statements the link between the capital account and the profit for the year was not shown.

(j)   The date on which the long-term loan is repayable is a useful piece of information.

(k)   The sales returns of £400 (item 35) has been deducted from sales. As with (e) it has not been disclosed.

(l)   The carriage in (item 21) has been included with purchases (item 29).

(m)   The employers' contribution to national insurance is a part of the cost of employing staff and it seems sensible to include it with wages. So wages (item 28) of £80,000 and employers' contribution (item 39) of £5,000 have been totalled to give £85,000. However, we have gone further and divided the wages expense between administrative and salesmens' wages.

(n)   Electricity (item 32) and gas (item 22) are both small and so they have been merged under the heading of light and heat.

(o)   As above, items 24 and 27 have been merged.

(p)   There are a number of very small expenses (items 19, 25, 31 and 37) and these have been included with sundry expenses.
(q)   All the vehicles are used by the salesmen.
(r)   Even though there is not a bank loan at the year-end it appears that there was a loan which was repaid during the year.

Horizontal Form

FRED

Balance Sheet as at 31 December 19X4

	£	£		£	£
Owners' capital account			*Fixed assets*		
Capital at 1 January 19X4		216,382	Freehold property,		
Profit for the year		30,223	at cost		150,000
			Motor vehicles,		
			at cost	20,000	
			less Accumulated		
			depreciation	14,000	6,000
		246,605			156,000
less Drawings		18,000			
		228,605	*Current assets*		
			Inventory at the lower		
			of cost and net		
Long-term loan			realizable value	80,000	
Repayable 1 January XX		40,000	Trade debtors less		
			provision against		
Current liabilities			doubtful debts	89,600	
Trade creditors	58,000		Prepaid expenses	1,700	
Accrued expenses	2,700	60,700	Balance at bank and		
			cash in hand	2,005	173,305
		£329,305			£329,305

Income Statement

Year ended 31 December 19X4

	£	£			£
Opening inventory		70,000	Sales		599,600
Purchases and carriage in		424,200			
		494,200			
less Closing inventory		80,000			
Cost of goods sold		414,200			
Gross profit c/d		185,400			
		£599,600			£599,600

Administrative expenses			Gross profit b/d	185,400
Administrative wages	53,000			
Rates	8,000			
Insurance	6,000			
Light and heat	5,000			
Printing, postage and				
stationery	3,620			
Sundry expenses	5,052	80,672		
Selling and distribution				
expenses				
Salesmens' wages	32,000			
Carriage out	15,000			
Advertising	18,000			
Salesmens' expenses	2,500			
Bad debts	705			
Depreciation of				
motor vehicles	2,000	70,205		
Financial expenses				
Interest on long-term				
loan	4,000			
Interest on bank loan	300	4,300		
		155,177		
Net profit		30,223		
		£185,400		£185,400

EXERCISES

9.1 Discuss the meaning and importance of working capital. It is often said that the 'ideal ratio' of current assets to current liabilities is 1·5 to 1. Comment on this view.

9.2 Why is 'materiality' so difficult to define, especially in so far as it relates to the items which should be disclosed separately in financial statements? It is sometimes argued that items should be considered material if they are greater than, say, 5 or 10 per cent of the net profit. Discuss this view and suggest alternatives.

9.3 The following trial balance was extracted from the books of George Rex as at 30 June 19X6.

Required:

(i) Show the journal entries necessary to record the adjustments required in respect of A1 to A8.

(ii) Prepare, in vertical form, Rex's income statement for the year ended 30 June 19X6 and his balance sheet as at that date.

	£		£
Advertising	740	Capital account	28,089
Carriage in	62	Loan	10,000
Carriage out	1,213	Motor vehicle,	
Cash in hand	17	accumulated	
Cost of goods sold	62,400	depreciation as at	
Drawings	12,000	1.7.X5	900
Entertaining (of customers)		Office equipment,	
expense	872	accumulated	
Freehold land and buildings	30,000	depreciation as at	
Interest on bank overdraft	164	1.7.X5	2,200
Insurance expenses	942	Overdraft	2,100
Insurance prepaid	60	Provision against	
Inventory	12,472	doubtful debts	300
Motor vehicle, at cost	2,000	Purchase ledger control	6,423
Motor vehicle expenses	831	Sales	110,400
National Insurance (employer's		Salesman's expenses	
contribution)	320	payable	42
Office equipment, at cost	4,000	Telephone charges	
Postage expense	210	payable	34
Printing expense	2,135	Wages payable	520
Rates expense	6,237		
Rates prepaid	1,862		
Repairs to office equipment	15		
Sales ledger control	6,400		
Salesman's expenses	1,218		
Subscriptions to a trade			
association	8		
Sundry expenses	3,460		
Telephone expense	218		
Wages expense	11,152		
	£161,008		£161,008

(A)   Adjustments are required in respect of the following:

1. Rex's book-keeper did not know how to deal with discounts allowed; so he ignored them, i.e. he credited the cash received to the sales ledger control account and personal accounts, but made no entries in respect of the discounts. Discounts allowed during the year amounted to £280.

2. Some office equipment was sold during the year. The proceeds, £120, were credited to the sales account but no other entry was made. The equipment sold had cost £1,000 and its net book value at 1 July 19X5 was £160.

3. The loan is from Rex's father. Rex paid his father £3,200 on 30 June
   19X6 of which £1,200 was interest for the year ended 30 June 19X6.
   The whole of the payment was credited to the loan account. The next
   repayment of principal is not due for another two years.

4. The balance on the sales ledger control account does not agree with the
   total of the sales ledger balances. An investigation revealed that bad
   debts of £500 had been written off the personal accounts but that no
   other entry had been made.

5. The provision against doubtful debts is to be maintained at 5 per cent
   of debtors.

6. Depreciation for the year is to be provided at the following rates
   Motor vehicle   25 per cent of cost
   Office equipment   10 per cent of cost.

7. In June Rex paid £1,800 for the printing of price lists for use in a sales
   campaign which is to start in September 19X6.

8. Prepaid insurance at 30 June 19X6 is £160 not £60.

(B)   You also learn that Rex has one salesman who is paid £3,800 per
       year. The motor vehicle is used by the salesman. £60 of the advertis-
       ing expense was spent on advertising for staff.

9.4 Len Shaw's accountant Sue Perb left on 1 January 19X4 and her
place was taken by a Miss Fitt. Miss Fitt produced the following income
statement for the year ended 31 December 19X4 and balance sheet as at
that date.

	£	£
Sales		260,900
less Accumulated depreciation as at 31 December 19X4		
– Motor vehicles	1,600	
– Shop fittings	1,800	
Advertising	8,500	
Bad debts – decrease in provision against doubtful debts	600	
Carriage in	2,800	
Carriage out	11,300	
Cost of goods sold	145,000	
	171,600	260,900

	£	£
	171,600	260,900
Coffee and milk (used for office coffees)	20	
Drawings	17,150	
Discounts received	1,200	
Donation paid to various local charities	2,350	
Light and heat	2,000	
Motor vehicle expenses	3,000	
Part-time typing	60	
Rates	9,000	
Rent	12,000	
School fees for Shaw's son	1,500	
Selling expenses	4,000	
Sundry expenses	3,120	
Wages	28,000	
	255,000	
less Sales returns	4,900	250,100
Profit for the year		£10,800

	£			£
Capital	12,730	Motor vehicles		3,200
Depreciation for 19X4		Inventory		14,000
– Motor vehicles	800	Sales ledger		
– Shop fittings	600	balances		19,600
Light and heat payable	400	Shop fittings		3,000
Overdraft	2,100	Difference		1,110
less Cash in hand	520 1,580			
Profit for 19X4	10,800			
Provision against doubtful				
debts	2,000			
Purchase ledger balances	9,400			
Rates prepaid	1,000			
Wages payable	1,600			
	£40,910			£40,910

Shaw feels that there may well be one or two things wrong with the above and he asks you to check the statements and to make a general examination of the accounting records. During the course of your investigations you discover the following:

1. Inventory at 31 December 19X4 should be £13,000.

2. A payment of £80 made for sundry expenses had not been posted.

3. Wages payable at the year end should be £1,420.

4. The sum included in the balance sheet as overdraft is the figure shown on the bank statement. Your bank reconciliation is as follows:

	£	£
Balance per bank statement 31 December X4		2,100 OD
add Cheques not yet presented	1,427	
	273	
	1,000	2,700
		4,800
less Receipts from credit customers not yet		
recorded in the cash book		3,200
		£1,600 OD

The payments represented by the cheques had all been debited to the appropriate accounts but the receipts, being cash received through the bank Giro system, had neither been recorded in the cash book nor posted to the appropriate accounts.

5. The total of the purchase ledger balance, £9,400 (the figure that was included in the balance sheet) does not agree with the balance of the purchase ledger control account, £9,780. You discover that the total of the purchase ledger balances had been undercast by £470 and that an error had been made when posting the March purchases to the purchase ledger control account. The total purchases for March were £10,210 and although the correct posting had been made to the inventory account, £10,120 was posted to purchase ledger control account.

Redraft the income statement and balance sheet in good form. Use the vertical form for both statements.

10 | Alternatives and the Worksheet

In this chapter we shall introduce the reader to some slightly different ways of doing the book-keeping and show how, in practice, a set of financial statements is prepared by using a worksheet.

First the alternatives.

MIXED ACCOUNTS

The point of difference is whether, for example, the 'expenses' and 'payables' should be dealt with in separate or in the same ledger accounts.

The system described so far keeps the 'expenses' and the 'payables'; and the 'expenses' and the 'prepaids', in different accounts. Thus we could describe each account as being 'pure' in that it is either an expense or a revenue, or an asset or a liability account and does not try to serve two functions.

The alternative is to combine, say, an expense and a payable in the same account. With this system the one account serves both as the springboard for a transfer to the income statement and as a record of the asset or liability. It is best to introduce such a 'mixed' account by way of an example.

Suppose the balance on a firm's electricity account at 31 December 19X2 is £600. The last entry in the account was the debiting of that account with the electricity bill which showed the charge up to 30 September 19X2. From a reading of the meter it is ascertained that 10,000 units have been used since 30 September, which at a cost of 2 pence per unit represents a charge of £200.

Under the 'pure' system we would deal with this by debiting an 'electricity expense' account with £200 and crediting an 'electricity payable' account with £200. In the 'mixed' system we do very much the same thing: we show the transfer to the income statement, which is the electricity

expense for the period, as being £600 + £200 = £800 and show the credit
balance as the electricity payable (or accrued) on the electricity account.

Electricity

		£			£
		600			
31 Dec	Balance c/d	200	31 Dec	Income statement	800
		£800			£800
			1 Jan	Balance b/d	200

We can best describe what we have done as follows: we know that we
want to transfer £800 to owners' equity (via the income statement) as being
the charge for the period. So let us do that first.

Electricity

			£
£			
600	31 Dec	Income statement	800

This transfer leaves a credit balance of £200 on the account and we show
this balance as being carried down in the normal way.

It is often easier to think of the amount that is owed (or prepaid)
first rather than the expense figure. So we often start with the required
balance:

Electricity

		£			£
		600			
31 Dec	Balance c/d	200			
		£800			
			1 Jan	Balance b/d	200

and then see that the required transfer is £800. But however we approach
the problem we arrive at the same result.

The following examples show the use of mixed accounts in other
situations.

Example 10.1 Expense/Prepayment

Reg started business on 1 January 19X4. On that date, he paid rates of £300 for the period 1 January 19X4 to 31 March 19X4. He also made the following payments for rates in the year ended 31 December 19X4.

| 1 March 19X4 | £800 for the period 1 March – 30 September 19X4 |
| 1 October 19X4 | £800 for the period 1 October 19X4 – 31 March 19X5 |

Rates

19X4		£	19X4		£
1 Jan	Cash	300	31 Dec	Income	
1 Mar	Cash	800		statement	1,500
1 Oct	Cash	800	31 Dec	Balance c/d	400
		£1,900			£1,900
19X5					
1 Jan	Balance b/d	400			

Example 10.2 Revenue/Debtor

On 1 January 19X4 Reg sublet a part of his shop to Frank at a rent of £10 per month. Frank paid Reg £50 on 1 June 19X4 and £40 on 1 November 19X4.

Rent Receivable

19X4		£	19X4		£
			1 Jun	Cash	50
31 Dec	Income statement	120	1 Nov	Cash	40
			31 Dec	Balance c/d	30
		£120			£120
19X5					
1 Jan	Balance b/d	30			

A Comparison of the Alternative Systems

The mixed system requires fewer ledger accounts and obviates the need for reversing entries. On the other hand, this system is not as suitable for the preparation of interim statements since the recognition of the asset/liability depends on the closing of the accounts, which is only done at the year-end.

The pure system tends to be used in the United States while the mixed system is, on the whole, favoured in the United Kingdom. However, many large firms in the United Kingdom have adopted the pure system not only because of its merits but also because of the spread of American practice caused by the acquisition of many British companies by American concerns.

INVENTORY AND PURCHASES ACCOUNTS

Another major alternative book-keeping practice is the use of purchases and stock accounts rather than cost of goods sold and inventory accounts. Stock (British terminology) and inventory (American jargon) mean the same thing but because the purchases/stock account method tends to be used in the United Kingdom we will use the word stock when describing this method.

As we have shown earlier the main feature of the inventory/cost of goods sold system is that the inventory account represents the asset while the cost of goods sold account represents the associated expense for the period. So we have a pure system: one account for the asset, and one for the expense.

The alternative approach has the features of a mixed system. The purchases account shows the cost of the goods purchased for resale during the period (and is, of course, neither an asset nor an expense) while the stock account represents the stock on hand the last time the books were balanced and financial statements prepared. An example of the purchases/ stock method is provided below.

To understand the purchases/stock method, let us take the example of a sole trader (Hall) whose year-end is 31 December. The relevant extract from Hall's trial balance as at 31 December 19X4 is:

	Debit	Credit
	£	
Stock	1,400	
Purchases	14,300	

The stock figure represents the goods on hand when financial statements were last prepared, 31 December 19X3, while the purchases balance shows the goods that have been purchased during the year.

The first step is to assume that the goods represented by both the opening stock and the purchases accounts have been used up, i.e. treat them as expenses. So the accounts will appear as follows:

Purchases

19X4	£	19X4	£
		31 Dec Trading	
Balance per trial balance	£14,300	account	£14,300

Stock

19X4		£	19X4		£
1 Jan	Balance	1,400	31 Dec	Trading account	1,400

We have annotated the transfer of the balances to owners' equity with the term trading account. This is because the items will be shown as expenses in the trading account section of the profit and loss account or income statement.

The purchases account is now closed as we have indicated by ruling it off.

However if, as is usual, Hall has some stock at the end of the year the expense 'cost of goods sold' will be overstated by the amount of that stock. This problem is dealt with by crediting the trading account (and hence owners' equity) with the amount of the closing stock (say it is £1,600) and debiting the stock account with that amount. The stock account will then be:

Stock

19X4		£	19X4		£
1 Jan	Balance	1,400	31 Dec	Trading account	1,400
31 Dec	Trading account	1,600	31 Dec	Balance c/d	1,600
		£3,000			£3,000
19X5					
1 Jan	Balance b/d	1,600			

Since it is an asset £1,600 will appear in the balance sheet.

The relevant extract from Hall's trading account for the year ended 31 December 19X4 is:

	£
Opening stock	1,400
Purchases	14,300
	15,700
less Closing stock	1,600
Cost of goods sold	£14,100

A Comparison of the Methods

With the purchases/stock method the recognition of the expense of cost of goods sold is essentially a year-end adjustment, so the other method is more suitable for firms wanting to prepare interim financial statements. The purchases/stock method is more widely used in the United Kingdom while the inventory/cost of sales method tends to be used by American firms; but as in the case of the pure/mixed ledger account alternatives, British firms are increasingly using the American method.

USING THE WORKSHEET

We shall conclude this chapter by presenting an extended example showing how a set of accounting statements can be prepared in practice, using the mixed ledger account and purchases/stock methods. We shall also stick to British terminology throughout the example.

Our example deals with the preparation of Fred Blank's profit and loss account for the year ended 31 December 19X4 and his balance sheet as at that date. The necessary work is often done on a worksheet. One form of worksheet is illustrated in Figure 10.1. At this stage, look at the headings of the columns and note that the first two columns consist of our old friend the trial balance.

Adjustments

Life would indeed be easy if the figures in the trial balance could simply be rearranged to give us the profit and loss account and balance sheet. But as you might suspect life is not easy.*

We have to make a number of adjustments in order to convert our dull old trial balance into a scintillating profit and loss account and balance sheet. Broadly the adjustments may be classified as follows:

general tidying up and the correction of errors;
the recognition of accruals and prepayments;
the inclusion of closing stock; and
the adjustment of the book value of assets
(i.e. depreciation, bad debts).

Tidying Up and the Correction of Errors

Often the work involved in the preparation of the financial statements will disclose a number of errors. Suppose that a purchase of stationery amounting to £60 had been debited by an absent-minded bookkeeper to the motor vehicles expense account. We deal with this by putting

---

* The use of the alternative method could obviate the need for a worksheet. See page 48.

Figure 10.1 Worksheet

	Trial Balance (Debit)	Trial Balance (Credit)	(Item)	Adjustments (Debit)	Adjustments (Credit)	Profit & Loss Account (Debit)	Profit & Loss Account (Credit)	Balance Sheet (Debit)	Balance Sheet (Credit)
	£	£		£	£	£	£	£	£
Balance at bank	1,100							1,100	
Capital		2,657							2,657
Cash in hand	25							25	
Drawings	4,590		(2)	10				4,600	
Electricity	69		(3)	21		90			
Insurance	110		(4)		40	70			
Motor van – at cost	800							800	
– accumulated depreciation		400	(6)		200				600
Motor vehicle expenses	180		(1)		60	120			
Postage and stationery	50		(1), (2)	60	10	100			
Provision against doubtful debts		150	(7)	100					50
Purchases	16,000					16,000			
Rates	350		(4)		75	275			
Rent – payable	500		(3)	100		600			
– receivable		42	(4)		10		52		
Sales		23,000					23,000		
Stock	150		(5)	1,200	1,200	150	1,200	1,200	
Sundry expenses	1,300					1,300			
Trade creditors		2,200							2,200
Trade debtors	1,000							1,000	
Wages	2,225		(3)	25		2,250			
Sundry creditors and accrued expenses			(3)		146				146
Sundry debtors and prepaid expenses			(4)	125				125	
Depreciation expense			(6)	200		200			
Bad debts			(7)		100		100		
	£28,449	£28,449		£1,841	£1,841	£21,155	£24,352	£8,850	£5,653
Difference, being the profit for the period						3,197			3,197
						£24,352	£24,352	£8,850	£8,850

£60 in the debit adjustment column against postage and stationery (thus increasing the expense) and £60 in credit adjustment column against motor vehicles expenses (reducing the expense). This is shown as item 1 in Figure 10.1.

Another type of adjustment will be required if any transactions escaped being recorded by the routine accounting system. Suppose the proprietor had used some stamps, purchased by the firm, for his private use and further suppose (a more unlikely assumption) he wished to record it. An estimate of the usage would be made, say £10, and it would be dealt with as follows:

	Adjustment Columns	
	Debit	Credit
Drawings	10	
Postage and stationery		10

(Item 2 in Figure 10.1)

Accruals and Prepayments

Basically we have to do three things:

1. Identify those expenses which have been incurred but which are yet to be paid or otherwise recognized (accrued expenses).
2. Identify those payments which represent expenses which should not be charged in the current period but rather in subsequent periods (prepaid expenses).
3. Identify any revenue which has not been recorded but which should be recognized in this period (debtors). Conservatism ensures that this is usually a short list.

The accountant examines the make-up of the figures in the ledger and uses his knowledge of the business to produce schedules of accrued expenses and of debtors and prepaid expenses.

Suppose that our in example it is discovered that:

— the rent is £50 per month but that it has only been paid to the end of October. Two months' rent, £100, is therefore to be accrued.

— the last electricity bill was paid in November on the basis of a meter reading 44,000 units, while at 31 December the reading was 46,300 units. Then if the charge per unit is 0·9 pence the amount to be accrued is £21. Some accountants would accrue £20.70 rather than rounding off; this is narrow-minded pedantry which should be avoided. In fact it is often possible and desirable to work to the nearest £10 or £100 when dealing with accruals and prepayments.

– 31 December was a Wednesday and, since the firm pays the wages on Friday, three days' wages amounting to £25 are due.

The accrued expenses schedule would then be:

	£
Rent payable	100
Electricity	21
Wages	25
	£146

The treatment of the above on the work sheet is shown as item 3 in Figure 10.1. The individual amounts are placed in the debit adjustment column against the appropriate accounts while the total is put in the credit adjustment column against a new entry which may be called 'sundry creditors and accrued expenses'. The result is that we have recorded the rent, electricity, and wages expenses, and have also recorded the amounts owed as a liability.

A similar operation would be carried out in respect of debtors and prepaid expenses. Say it is discovered that:

– the last rates payment was for the six months ended 31 March next and amounted to £150.

– all the firm's insurance premiums are paid for a year in advance on 30 June and the last payment was £80.

– the firm lets a part of the yard to a local barrow boy to store his barrow. The charge is £1 per week and as at 31 December the barrow boy owed the firm £10.

The debtors' and prepayments' schedule would be:

	£
Rates	75
Insurance	40
Rent receivable	10
	£125

The individual amounts would be placed in the credit adjustment column while the total would be put in the debit adjustment column and described as 'sundry debtors and prepaid expenses' or some such title. This is illustrated in item 4 of Figure 10.1.

The Inclusion of Closing Stock

The figure shown in the trial balance as stock represents the stock at the start of the period. This will be charged, without adjustment, to the income statement as part of the cost of goods sold.

The closing stock has to be counted and entered. It has two effects in the financial statements. In the trading account it reduces the cost of goods sold (a credit entry) and on the balance sheet it appears as an asset (a debit). So we do a rather strange thing on our worksheet: we put the closing stock, say it is £1,200, in both the debit and credit adjustment columns against stock (see item 5 in Figure 10.1). The credit entry reminds us to include the closing stock in the trading account; the debit entry ensures that the stock is included in the balance sheet.

Adjusting the Book Value of Assets

Depreciation   The depreciation charge for the year has been computed at £200. We deal with this by adding a new line to our worksheet called depreciation expense (we will find that we need a depreciation expense account) and show £200 in the debit adjustment column against depreciation expense and £200 in the credit adjustment column against accumulated depreciation (item 6).

Provision against Doubtful Debts   If the balance on the provision account is considered reasonable, no adjustment is required. But suppose the provision is considered to be excessive: say it is thought that it should be reduced from £150 to £50.

As with depreciation we need to add an extra line to the worksheet. We could call it bad debts. The adjustment is reflected by entering £100 in the debit adjustment column against provision against doubtful debt accounts, thus reducing that balance to the required amount, and putting £100 in the credit adjustment column against bad debts (item 7).

Since the balance on the bad debts account is a credit, it will be shown on the profit and loss account as 'reduction in provision against doubtful debts'.

The more perceptive of our readers may have realized that we have always ensured that the debit entries equalled the credit entries. It is a useful check to cast the debit and credit adjustment columns to see that the totals are equal.

Profit and Loss Account and Balance Sheet Columns

We can now breathe a sigh of satisfaction if we think that we have done all the necessary adjusting entries, or start worrying if we think that we have left some out. However, we must move on: note that the penultimate pair of columns is labelled profit and loss account while the last pair is described as the balance sheet. Our aim is to put all the revenue and expense items in the profit and loss account columns and the assets, liabilities and owners' equity balance in the balance sheet columns. If this is done our task is completed, since we have now arrived at a profit and loss account and a balance sheet. All the figures are in the appropriate columns; all we have to do is rewrite the statements in logical, meaningful and conventional form.

There is a difference between the totals of each pair of columns. The credit total in the profit and loss account pair exceeds the debit total by £3,197. This is the amount by which revenue exceeds the expenses and is the profit for the period.

The difference between the totals of the balance sheet columns must also be £3,197, but this time it is the debit total which is larger. The profit figure serves as a link between the statements, for when the profit is added to owners' equity the credit side will be increased and we have that most pleasing of sights, a balance sheet that balances.

FRED BLANK
Profit and Loss Account
for the year ended 31 December 19X4

	£	£	£
Sales			23,000
less Opening stock		1,300	
Purchases		16,000	
		17,300	
less Closing stock		1,200	16,100
Gross profit			6,900
less Wages		2,250	
Rent payable		600	
Rates		275	
Postage and stationery		100	
Electricity		90	
Insurance		70	
Motor vehicle expenses		120	
Depreciation of motor vehicle		200	
Sundry expenses		150	
		3,855	
less Rent receivable	52		
Reduction in provision against doubtful debts	100	152	3,703
Profit for the year			£3,197

Foundation in Accounting

Balance Sheet at 31 December 19X4

	£	£	£
Fixed assets			
Motor van at cost		800	
less Depreciation charged to date		600	200
Current assets			
Stock at cost		1,200	
Trade debtors, less provision against doubtful debts		950	
Sundry debtors and prepaid expenses		125	
Balance at bank and cash in hand		1,125	
		3,400	
less **Current liabilities**			
Trade creditors	2,200		
Sundry creditors and accrued expenses	146	2,346	1,054
			£1,254
Capital account			
Opening balance			2,657
add Profit for the year			3,197
			5,854
less Drawings			4,600
			£1,254

*   *   *

Meanwhile, Back at the Ledger

The financial statements being completed, you might feel that you are due for a rest, but there is one more task to be done. We must return to the ledger and record therein the adjustments included in the work sheets and perform the time-honoured ceremony of closing the books.

The first step is to deal with the general tidying up entries described earlier. These will be recorded in the journal and posted to the ledger accounts in the usual way. The depreciation expense and the adjustment to the provision against doubtful debts are also dealt with through journal entries.

The revenue and expense accounts which are, as you remember, temporary owners' equity accounts, are dealt with by transferring the revenue and expenses for the period to the owners' capital account. The drawings account is also a temporary owners' equity, so this too is transferred to capital account.

The balances representing the assets, liabilities and owners' equity are now carried down.

The Opening Trial Balance

The end is, at last, in sight! We have brought down balances on the asset, liability and owners' equity accounts, and these constitute the balance sheet. (This may not always be obvious since there is some aggregation on the balance sheet.) In fact the balance sheet may be defined as a statement of the balances remaining on the ledger accounts after the closure of the revenue and expense accounts.

These balances also give us the starting position for the next accounting period; so it is a good idea to check that they are correct. To do this we prepare (outside the ledger) an opening trial balance which lists the opening balances which are on the ledger accounts and ensure that:

the debits equal the credits, and
that the figures agree with the balance sheet.

We show below the necessary journal entries and the opening trial balance:

The Journal

(a) General tidying up entries

Date		Fo.	£	£
31 Dec X4	Postage and stationery	P1	60	
	Motor vehicle expenses	M3		60
	Being the correction of an allocation error Fo. *x* of cash book.			
31 Dec X4	Drawings	D1	10	
	Postage and stationery	P1		10
	Being the estimated private use of stamps.			

(b) Depreciation and doubtful debts

Date		Fo.	£	£
31 Dec X4	Depreciation expense	D2	200	
	Motor van — accumulated depreciation	M2		200
	Being the depreciation charge for the year.			
31 Dec X4	Provision against doubtful debts	P2	100	
	Bad debts	B1		100
	Being the required reduction in the provision against doubtful debts			

(c) The closing of revenue and expense accounts

Date		Fo.	£	£
31 Dec X4	Bad debts	B1	100	
	Rent — receivable	R3	52	
	Sales	S1	23,000	
	Stock account	S2	1,200	
	Depreciation expense	D2		200 .
	Electricity	E1		90
	Insurance	I1		70
	Motor vehicle expenses	M3		120
	Postage and stationery	P1		100
	Purchases	P3		16,000
	Rates	R1		275
	Rent — payable	R2		600
	Stock account	S2		1,300
	Sundry expenses	S3		150
	Wages	W1		2,250
	Capital account, being the profit for the year	C1		3,197
			£24,352	£24,352*

* The totals are not strictly necessary but they are a useful check for long journal entries.

(d) Owners' equity accounts

Date		Fo.	£	£
31 Dec X4	Capital account	C1	4,800	
	Drawings	D1		4,800
	Being the transfer of the owners' drawings for the period			

(e) Accrued and prepaid expenses

These adjustments are, with the particular method outlined, not normally recorded in the journal.

The Opening Trial Balance

	£	£
Capital account		1,254
Electricity		21
Insurance	40	
Motor van – at cost	800	
– accumulated depreciation		600
Provision against doubtful debts		50
Rates	75	
Rent – payable		100
– receivable	10	
Stock	1,200	
Trade creditors		2,200
Trade debtors	1,000	
Wages		25
Cash book	1,100	
Petty cash book	25	
	£4,250	£4,250

EXERCISES

10.1 There are no scarce resources on Mars, hence Martians have no need for, or knowledge of, accounting. Xerak, a recently arrived Martian with a perfect knowledge of English, asks you to explain to him, as concisely as possible, the nature and purposes of income statements and balance sheets.

10.2 J. Duke started business on 1 January 19X2 (his year-end being 31 December). Show how the following would be recorded in Duke's

ledger for the period 1 January 19X2 to 31 December 19X3; bring down
balances as at 31 December each year, using:

(a) The pure system; and

(b) The mixed system.

1. *Electricity*

Date bill received	Date bill paid	Period covered by bill	Amount £
6 Apr 19X2	13 May 19X2	1 Jan 19X2 – 31 Mar 19X2	40
10 Oct 19X2	12 Nov 19X2	1 Apr 19X2 – 30 Sep 19X2	90
11 Apr 19X3	10 Jun 19X3	1 Oct 19X2 – 31 Mar 19X3	100
15 Oct 19X3	1 Dec 19X3	1 Apr 19X3 – 30 Sep 19X3	120

Estimated cost of electricity consumed in period:

    1 October 19X2 – 31 December 19X2 £48
    1 October 19X3 – 31 December 19X3 £57

2. *Insurance*

Duke paid the following insurance premiums:

	Date paid	Amount £	Period covered
Policy A	10 Jan 19X2	100	1 Jan 19X2 – 31 Dec 19X2
Policy B	5 Jul 19X2	200	1 Jul 19X2 – 30 Jun 19X3
Policy C	2 Jan 19X3	600	1 Nov 19X2 – 31 Oct 19X3
Policy A	5 Jan 19X3	110	1 Jan 19X3 – 31 Dec 19X3
Policy B	7 Jul 19X3	220	1 Jul 19X3 – 30 Jun 19X4
Policy C	10 Nov 19X3	660	1 Nov 19X3 – 31 Oct 19X4

3. *Rent*

Duke rented a property on 1 July 19X2 at a rental of £100 per month. He
subsequently made the following rental payments:

Date paid	Amount £
1 July 19X2	400
10 December 19X2	300
1 July 19X3	500
1 November 19X3	200

10.3 The trial balance as at 31 December 19X2 of J. Parrot, a trader, is given below:

Debit		*Credit*	
Stock	20,000	Capital account	56,000
Freehold property,		Sales	153,000
at cost	30,000	Fixtures and fittings	
Fixtures and fittings		accumulated depreciation	7,000
at cost	10,000	Creditors' control account	12,000
Salaries and wages	18,000	Bank overdraft	10,000
Insurance	3,000		
Advertising	16,000		
Sundry expenses	12,000		
Debtors' control account	38,000		
Purchases	86,000		
Drawings	5,000		
	£238,000		£238,000

The following information is relevant:

1. Stock, at cost, at 31 December 19X2 was £25,000.

2. The depreciation charge for fixtures and fittings for the year is 10 per cent on cost.

3. Salaries and wages owing at 31 December 19X2 amounted to £2,000.

4. Prepaid insurance at 31 December 19X2 was £1,000.

5. Included in sundry expenses was £7,000 spent on the construction of an additional door and staircase in Parrot's freehold premises.

6. Parrot does not want to establish a provision against doubtful debts account but does wish to write off bad debts amounting to £6,000.

7. Parrot conducted an extensive advertising campaign in November and December 19X2. It has not been paid for (or otherwise reflected in his books) and it is thought that the cost will be £30,000. Of this expenditure it is considered that £25,000 relates to 19X3.

(a) Complete a worksheet starting with the above trial balance and incorporating the above adjustments; prepare Parrot's profit and loss account for the year ended 31 December 19X2 and his balance sheet as at that date.

(b) Comment on Parrot's method of accounting for bad debts.

(c) Outline the arguments for and against writing off the whole of the cost of the advertising campaign in 19X2.

10.4 The 31 December 19X4 unadjusted trial balance of E. Blink, a trader, is given below:

Debit	£	Credit	£
Balance at bank	2,000	Interest on investment	100
Advertising	600	Discounts	2,400
Salaries and wages	19,400	Provision against	
Investments at cost	8,700	doubtful debts	3,000
Cash in hand	300	Long-term loan	20,000
Debtors' control account	46,800	Accumulated depreciation	
Insurance	1,300	– fixtures and fittings	8,000
Stock, 1 January 19X4	44,000	– motor vehicles	3,000
Freehold property	38,000	Creditors' control account	20,400
Carriage inwards	18,000	Sales	335,800
Carriage outwards	64,000	Capital account	103,550
Packaging materials	9,000		
Sales returns	6,350		
Drawings	12,000		
Sundry expenses	8,000		
Interest on long-term loan,			
6 months to 30.6.X4	1,000		
Auditors' remuneration	1,400		
Salesmens' expenses	10,000		
Legal fees	800		
Fixtures and fittings,			
at cost	14,000		
Rates	4,000		
Light and heat	3,700		
Postage and stationery	1,900		
Motor vehicles, at cost	8,000		
Purchases	172,200		
Discounts	800		
	£496,250		£496,250

The following adjustments have to be made:

1. The investment is a temporary one which Blink intends to dispose of soon. Its market value at 31 December 19X4 was £7,500.

2. Prepaid expenses at 31 December 19X4:

	£
Insurance	400
Rates	1,100

3. Accrued expenses at 31 December 19X4:

	£
Salaries and wages	600
Interest on loan	1,000
Legal fees	400
Light and heat	480

4. Stock of goods for resale at 31 December 19X4, at cost, £48,000. The net realizable value of a number of items was less than cost. Their aggregate cost was £6,000 and their total net realizable value £2,500.

5. Depreciation for the year is to be based on the following rates:

   Motor vehicles, 25 per cent of cost.
   Fixtures and fittings, 20 per cent of the reducing balance.

6. Packaging materials on hand at 31 December 19X4 at cost, £1,500.

7. Because Blink paid a number of his suppliers in advance there were a number of creditors' accounts with debit balances. The total of the debit balance was £4,000.

8. Of the cash float of £300 shown above, £200 was represented by advances made to salesmen against expenses. It is discovered that of this, £150 was spent by salesmen in December 19X4, while the balance represents payments, in advance, of their expenses in 19X5.

9. Blink agreed that certain invoices sent to customers in December 19X4 were incorrect. In total the customers had been overcharged by £2,000.

10. Blink had sold a motor vehicle for £1,200. The amount had been credited to the sales account but no other adjustment had been made. The vehicle was purchased on 1 January 19X2 for £2,000.

11. Bad debts of £1,800 are to be written off and the provision against doubtful debts is to be made equal to 5 per cent of the debtors.

12. 60 per cent of the salaries and wages were paid to salesmen and it is estimated that 20 per cent of the sundry expenses related to the sales department.

(a) Using a worksheet, record the above adjustments and hence prepare, in good form, Blink's profit and loss account for the year ended 31 December 19X4 and his balance sheet as at that date.

(b) Show the necessary correcting and closing journal entries.

(c) Show the following ledger accounts starting with the balance per trial balance:

stock, packaging materials, rates, light and heat.

(N.B. Use the mixed ledger account system).

Epilogue

We have attempted to show in this book the operation of the 'historical cost' accounting model in the context of a very simple form of business enterprise – a retailing, sole trader. Further studies in accountancy will involve more complex forms of enterprise – manufacturers, bankers, etc. – and more complex forms of business structure such as nationalized industries, limited companies and partnerships. These studies will show that, although there may be more practical difficulties in using the model in these cases, the basic principles hold.

But the traditional, historical-cost accounting model also needs to be further examined and so, before letting our readers go, we would like to provide one or two pointers which we hope might be of help to you when you move on to higher things. This discussion should also assist you in understanding some of the developments in accounting practice that are currently taking place.

The problems that are being examined at the moment may be summarized under three interrelated headings:

1. The variety of accounting practices;
2. The validity of the assumptions underlying the traditional accounting model, and;
3. Whether there may be more appropriate models than the traditional one for some or all purposes, e.g., current value accounting or cash flow accounting.

To take the points in turn.

VARIETY IN ACCOUNTING PRACTICES

We have shown in this book several examples where there are a number of ways of recording a given transaction; depreciation and the costing of inventory are particularly good examples, but there are many others. In general they arise when the accountant has to deal with uncompleted transactions. In many cases uncompleted transactions constitute a large proportion of the activities of the firm and this is particularly true for interim accounts, since the shorter the time period the larger the number of uncompleted transactions.

Essentially, the problem caused by the variety of practices is that it makes it difficult to compare the results of different firms if they select different methods, as indeed they do.

Another problem is that a firm can select the methods that yield the results that they desire. This is not such a large problem as it might be because of the rule followed by professional accountants that when a firm changes its accounting methods, the fact should be stated in a note to the financial statements, and the effect of the change on the results of the year should be given. But, of course, this still means that by a judicious change in accounting method the profits of the next few years can be increased, or decreased, from the level that would have been disclosed using the old methods. However, this process can only be carried out over a relatively short time, because in the end the transaction will be completed and, at that time, the results of the different treatments of the transaction will be the same. For example, a switch from accelerated depreciation to straight-line depreciation just before a company engages in an extensive investment programme would mean that the reported profits in the early years of the ownership of the assets would be higher than they would have been if the old method had been retained. However, since the income statement must ultimately be charged with the difference between the cost of an asset and any sales proceeds, the increased profits in the early years will be offset by decreased profits in the later years of the asset's life.

Accountants have been attacked in recent years because of the large number of different methods that were considered to be generally acceptable and in 1970 the Accounting Standards Steering Committee (ASSC) was established. The committee is made up of representatives of the major accountancy bodies in the United Kingdom and is not in any sense a government agency. Indeed, it has been suggested that one of the reasons behind its establishment was to forestall possible government intervention in this field.

The ASSC is carrying out a programme of examining various problem areas in an attempt to lay down 'statements of best accounting practice' or, as they are called, Statements of Standard Accounting Practice. The various professional bodies comprising the ASSC expect their members to ensure that any financial statements with which they are concerned either comply with these statements or that any departures from the methods laid down in these statements are explained.

The Financial Accounting Standards Board (FASB) is carrying out a similar programme in the United States although in that country a government agency, the Securities Exchange Commission (SEC) plays a significant part in the regulation of accounting practices.

THE VALIDITY OF THE ASSUMPTIONS UNDERLYING
THE TRADITIONAL MODEL

Currently the assumption that is being attacked most is that of the stable money unit. The conventional model assumes that pounds of different dates may be treated as units of equal value. Clearly this assumption is totally unrealistic; to add pounds of 1975 to pounds of 1935 is as meaningless as the addition of francs and marks or apples and pears.

For many years accountants, while recognizing the limitations of accounts based on historical cost, believed that there was no acceptable way of overcoming the problem caused by the stable money convention. For example, the Council of the Institute of Chartered Accountants in England and Wales in 1952 stated that:

> ... the alternatives to historical cost which have so far been suggested appear to have serious defects and their logical application would raise social and economic issues going far beyond the realm of accountancy. The Council is therefore unable to regard any of the suggestions so far made as being acceptable alternatives to the existing accounting principles based on historical cost.*

Progress has been made, accelerated by an inflation rate of over 20 per cent, and the Institute of Chartered Accountants is now a party to a Provisional Statement of Standard Accounting Practice entitled 'Accounting for Changes in the Purchasing Power of Money'.

The statement suggests that certain types of business organization (limited companies whose shares are quoted on the Stock Exchange) should publish, in addition to the usual accounts, supplementary financial statements. The distinguishing feature of these statements is that the assumption of the stable money unit is removed. This means that all costs, etc., are restated in pounds of current purchasing power. This approach takes account of changes in the general purchasing power of money but does not attempt to incorporate the current value of assets. Thus the historical cost approach is maintained but the supplementary statements are in terms of 'converted' costs instead of actual costs.

OTHER MODELS

Current purchasing power has arrived and, in conclusion, we should peer over the horizon to see what other developments are likely.

Many academic accountants, and some practising ones, argue that financial statements should be based on current values rather than the historical cost. In this model the balance sheet would be a statement showing the

---

*Recommendations on Accounting Principles, N15. Institute of Chartered Accountants in England and Wales, 1952.

current values of the assets less liabilities. The use of such an approach was proposed in the report of the Sandilands Committee†, which was established by the Government to consider the problems involved in accounting for changing prices. Under these proposals, profit would be the excess of sales revenue over the current costs of the related inputs.

There are those who argue that it is cash that counts and that we should cut through all the problems that surround the various accounting conventions and sidestep the valuation problems inherent in current value accounting by making the cash flow statement the prime instrument of financial accounting. The cash flow statement would show in some detail a firm's cash flows in and out for the period. It is suggested that the cash flow statement for the period should be accompanied by the cash flow statements a number of past periods as well as budgeted cash flow statements for future periods. While many would agree with the importance of cash flow statements as supplementary information, the view that they should completely replace the income statement and balance sheet is not widely held.

The question of what is the best basis for the preparation of financial statements is unlikely to be resolved for some considerable time – not until the fundamental question of deciding on the proper objectives behind the preparation and presentation of financial statements is settled. This has been, and is being attempted by various groups and individuals, but agreement will not come early or easily.

It would not be rash to wager that there will be considerable changes in financial accounting in the next few decades, but an even safer bet would be to say that double-entry book-keeping will survive for a long time yet and that many future generations of students will have to learn to grapple with their debits and credits.

---

†'Inflation Accounting – Report of the Inflation Accounting Committee'.
HMSO 1975, Cmnd 6225.

Index